Crayola®

create it yourself

Crayola®

CIY™

create it yourself

52

Colorful DIY Craft Projects
for Kids to Create
Throughout the Year

BLACK DOG
& LEVENTHAL
PUBLISHERS
NEW YORK

Black Dog & Leventhal Publishers
Hachette Book Group
1290 Avenue of the Americas
New York, NY 10104

www.hachettebookgroup.com
www.blackdogandleventhal.com

First Edition: October 2020

Interior photographs © Crayola
Interior photography by Patrick Shuck, by FGX Creative, LLC

Black Dog & Leventhal Publishers is an imprint of Perseus Books, LLC, a subsidiary of Hachette Book Group, Inc. The Black Dog & Leventhal Publishers name and logo are trademarks of Hachette Book Group, Inc.

The publisher is not responsible for websites (or their content) that are not owned by the publisher.

The Hachette Speakers Bureau provides a wide range of authors for speaking events. To find out more, go to www.HachetteSpeakersBureau.com or call (866) 376-6591.

Print book interior design by Katie Benezra and Ashley Prine, Tandem Books.

ISBNs: 978-0-7624-7069-3 (paperback), 978-0-7624-7188-1 (ebook)

Printed in China

APS

10 9 8 7 6 5 4 3 2 1

CONTENTS

SPRING

SUMMER

FALL

WINTER

INTRODUCTION

As a designer, I believe everything starts and ends with color. I see color in everything, and it always inspires me to create. I always say that surrounding one's life with color can bring everyone great joy and happiness.

I have always loved to draw. The range of colors inside a box of Crayola Crayons represents a world of possibilities to me. It's hard for me to pick just one favorite color because they're all so fabulous, but if I had to, mine would be Shocking Pink.

My lifelong love of color and design prompted a new and exciting collaboration with my friends at Crayola: Isaac Mizrahi Loves Crayola. I was thrilled to write the introduction for this wonderful book that celebrates color while encouraging creativity and memory making with family and friends.

Crayola launched a Create It Yourself (CIY) digital content network to give families a great way to engage with clever, colorful, and easy-to-make DIY crafts any time of the year. This book contains 52 of the most popular projects from the platform. My personal favorite is the iron-on Fabric Patches craft on page 118, because I love to add personal flair to everything I wear.

The Crayola team and I hope you find this book a great opportunity to encourage creativity and make memories that will last a lifetime.

Happy creating!
xo,

Isaac Mizrahi

HOW TO USE THIS BOOK

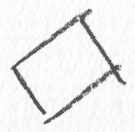

WELCOME TO A YEAR OF CREATIVITY with *Crayola CIY: Create It Yourself!* This book gives you and your kids 52 fun projects to make as the seasons change. You'll create gifts, decorations, and keepsakes that are as much fun to make as they are to give away.

Projects are intended for ages six and up with a little help from adults along the way. Some can be made by even younger kids than that, and most will entertain kids who are well into their tweens. If adult help is required regardless of the child's age, you'll see an "Adult Supervision Required" note under the craft title. Be sure to read through all instructions before starting kids out on a project to make sure it's appropriate for your unique little crafter.

Almost all of the projects can be created with basic crafting supplies, such as paint, scissors, glue, and of course crayons! We recommend using Crayola products where indicated so you know the projects will come out right.

The steps are simple, and the photographs will show kids just what they need to do. Videos for all the projects are also available on Crayola.com/crafts and the Crayola YouTube channel. Just search for the craft's name to find the tutorial.

So take a spin through the year and learn how to create a suncatcher for springtime, sparklers for the summer, a spooky cauldron for the fall, and a snow globe for winter!

SPRING

Spring into warmer weather with a DIY Puffy Paint Rainbow, Easter Egg Ornaments, and a Mother's Day Wreath. These crafts are great ways to stay busy while April showers are bringing May flowers.

PAPER BAG STAR

Make enchanting decorations with this colorful upcycled craft that transforms brown paper bags into hanging stars!

SUPPLIES:

- 8 paper bags
- Crayola Washable Paint
- Crayola Paintbrush
- Crayola Glue Stick
- Crayola Scissors
- Hole punch
- Ribbon

STEPS:

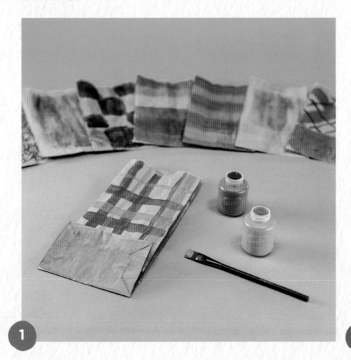

1. Decorate the large front (the front is the side where the bottom folds up) and bottom panels of all eight paper bags using paints. Let the paint dry for 1 hour.

2. Paint a design on the large back panel of each bag, and let the paint dry for 1 hour.

3

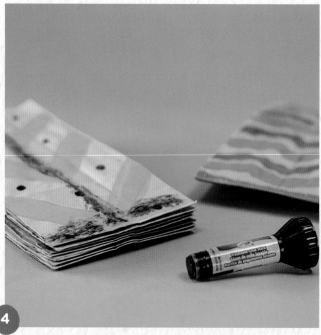

4

5

6

3. Follow the same process on both side panels of each bag, allowing for 1 hour of drying time in between.

4. Lay a folded, decorated paper bag flat with the open end at the top. Make an upside-down T on the large back panel (the one that doesn't have the bottom flap) with the glue stick. Put another paper bag on top, oriented the same way, and press down. Repeat with the remaining bags.

5. With scissors, cut a point at the open end of the paper bag stack.

6. Make an upside-down T with the glue stick on the last bag on the stack. Gently fan the paper bags, then press together the first and last paper bag to glue them together and create a paper star.

7. Use the hole punch to make a hole in the top of the paper star, then feed the ribbon through and tie it.

8. Hang the star as a party decoration or everyday décor!

DIY FISH TANK

Using Crayola Model Magic and other simple supplies, you can create an amazing aquarium craft with fish you'll never have to feed!

ADULT SUPERVISION REQUIRED

SUPPLIES:

- Glass jar with cork lid
- Crayola Washable Paint
- Crayola Paintbrush
- Crayola Model Magic®
- Three different sized paper clips
- Crayola Scissors
- Crayola No. 2 Pencil
- Crayola Construction Paper, green
- Crayola Washable No-Run School Glue

STEPS:

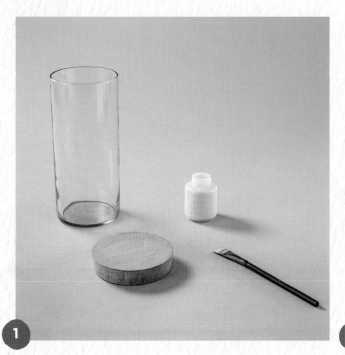

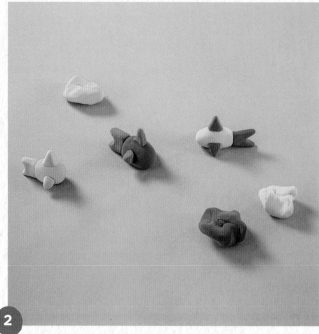

1. Paint the bottom and sides of the cork lid with yellow paint. Set aside to dry for 1–2 hours. After the paint is dry, paint a second coat.

2. Mold some fish out of different colors of Crayola Model Magic. We made three.

3. Unbend the paper clips so they're straight. Use various sizes of paper clips to make them different lengths.

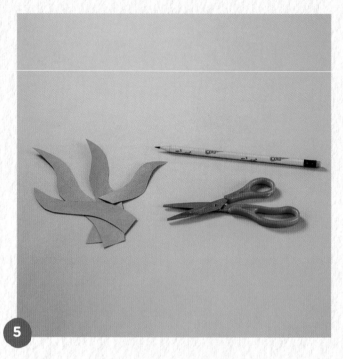

4. Stick one end of a paper clip into the bottom of a fish. Then, stick the other end of the paper clip into the bottom of the cork lid to secure.

5. Make seaweed by drawing wavy lines with a pencil on a piece of green construction paper and cutting out the shape with scissors.

6. Fold the bottom of the seaweed to create a tab. Apply a small amount of glue to the tab and attach it to the bottom of the cork lid to surround the fish.

7. Carefully place the jar upside down on top of the cork lid. Paint a wave of blue paint around the top of the jar to create "water."

PUFFY PAINT RAINBOW

Make a colorful puffy paint rainbow that will entice even the sneakiest leprechaun!

SUPPLIES:

- Crayola Color Glue, blue, green, yellow, and red
- Crayola Washable No-Run School Glue
- Disposable cups
- Measuring cups
- Foaming shaving cream
- Craft sticks
- Crayola Paintbrushes
- Cardstock
- Crayola No. 2 Pencil
- Crayola Construction Paper
- Crayola Scissors
- Crayola Glitter Glue

STEPS:

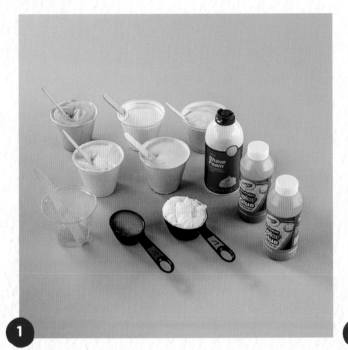

1

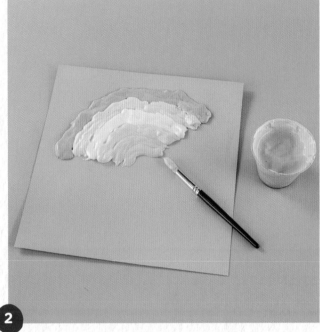

2

1. Refrigerate the Crayola Color Glue and Crayola Washable No-Run School Glue overnight. In a disposable cup, combine ¼ cup of color glue with ½ cup of foaming shaving cream and stir with a craft stick until fully mixed. Continue to create all of the colors of the rainbow.

2. Paint the glue mixtures onto a piece of cardstock to create a rainbow shape.

CIY STAFF TIP!

You will need to combine two colors of Crayola Color Glue to make certain colors. Mix yellow and red to get orange and blue and red to make purple.

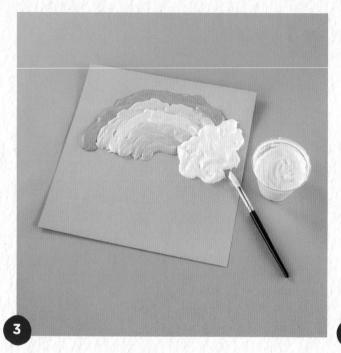

3

4

3. In another disposable cup, combine ¼ cup Crayola Washable No-Run School Glue with ½ cup foaming shaving cream and stir until fully mixed. Use this glue mixture to paint a fluffy white cloud at the end of your rainbow.

4. Using a pencil, draw the outline of a pot of gold on a piece of construction paper. Cut out the pot of gold and glue it to the end of your colorful rainbow.

5. Add shiny gold coins to your creation using glitter glue.

6. Once your project is dry, enjoy the fun, fluffy feeling of your rainbow.

CIY STAFF TIP! Experiment with more shaving cream for an even fluffier mixture.

5

DIY PAPER SPINNERS

Turn cardboard and string into twirly, whirly fun using Crayola Markers and Crayola Colored Pencils.

HELP FROM ADULTS

Kids will need help cutting out the cardboard disk in step 5 and poking holes through the spinner in step 7.

SUPPLIES:

- Crayola Colored Pencils
- Circular object (such as a coffee can)
- Crayola Construction Paper
- Crayola Markers
- Crayola Scissors
- Scrap cardboard (such as a cereal box)
- Crayola Glue Stick
- String
- Ruler

STEPS:

1. Using a pencil, trace around the bottom of a circular object onto construction paper. Repeat so you have two circles.

2. Draw designs inside the circles using markers and colored pencils.

3. Cut out the circles with scissors.

4. Place one of the circles onto a piece of scrap cardboard and trace.

5. Cut out the cardboard disc and attach a circle to each side of the cardboard disc using a glue stick.

6. Make two holes near the center of the cardboard disc, about ½ inch apart.

7. Cut a piece of string approximately 30 inches long.

8. Thread the string ends through the holes in the cardboard disc and tie the ends together.

9. Center the disc on the string. Hold the ends of the string and "flip" the disc repeatedly (like a jump rope) to wind up the spinner. Quickly pull the string taut to watch it swirl and twirl!

CIY STAFF TIPS!

Try designing your spinner with other art tools like Crayola Crayons or Crayola Washable Paint.
You can poke holes in the spinner using the point of a pen that has dried out or a paperclip.

DIY BUBBLE WRAP STAMPING

Here are three ways to upcycle leftover Bubble Wrap into awesome stamps.

HELP FROM ADULTS

Small children may need help cutting the paper towel tube in half in step 1.

SUPPLIES:

- Paper towel tube
- Crayola Scissors
- Bubble Wrap
- Rubber band
- Crayola Washable Paint
- Disposable plates
- Cardstock
- Crayola Markers
- Crayola Paintbrush
- Crayola No. 2 Pencil
- Cardboard
- Crayola Glue Stick

STEPS:

1. Cut a paper towel tube in half.

2. Cut out a piece of Bubble Wrap large enough to cover one end of the tube.

3. Secure the Bubble Wrap onto the end of the tube using a rubber band.

4. Pour two or three colors of paint onto a disposable plate so the paints touch.

5. Dip the Bubble Wrap end of the tube into the paint, getting a little of each color onto the Bubble Wrap.

6. Gently stamp a piece of cardstock, making pictures or patterns. We made a caterpillar.

7. Use markers to fill in some details, and voilà! A Bubble-Wrap-a-pillar.

BIG STAMP STEPS:

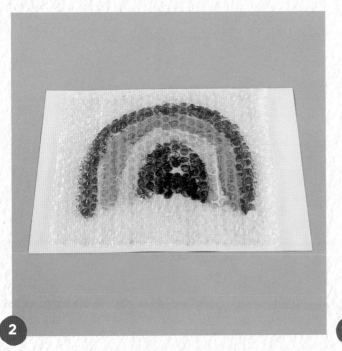

2

3

1. Using a paintbrush, paint a picture onto a piece of Bubble Wrap. We chose a rainbow.

2. Flip the Bubble Wrap over and gently press it onto cardstock.

3. Use markers to color in some details, and then admire your handiwork.

CIY STAFF TIP!

When you use the stamps, be sure to lower them gently to preserve the bubbly details.

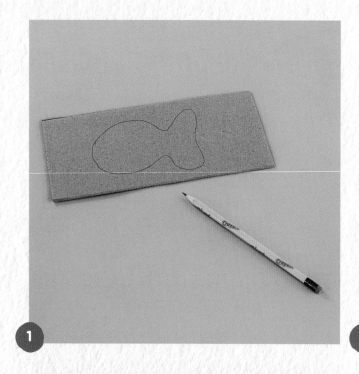

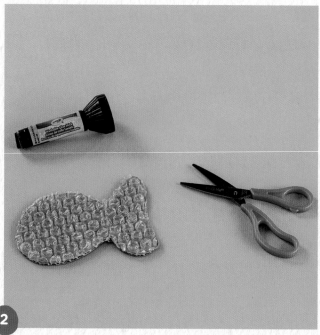

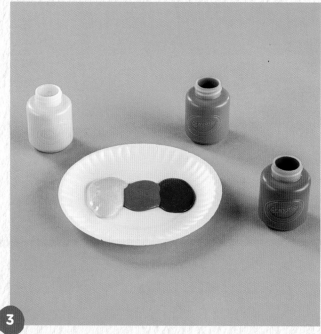

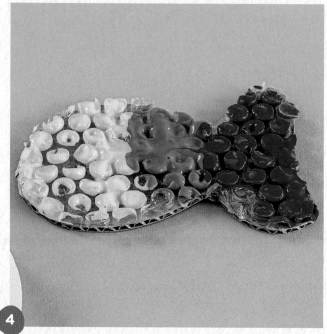

SHAPED STAMP STEPS:

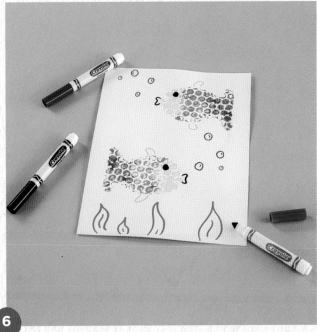

1. Using a pencil, draw a simple shape onto a piece of cardboard. We made a fish.

2. Cut out the shape with scissors. Attach a piece of Bubble Wrap to the cardboard shape using a glue stick. Cut out the Bubble Wrap around the cardboard shape.

3. Pour two or three colors of paint onto a disposable plate so the paints touch.

4. Dip the Bubble Wrap side of the shape into the paint, getting a little of each color onto the Bubble Wrap.

5. Gently stamp a piece of cardstock.

6. Use markers to color in some details, like some bubbles for your Bubble Wrap fish.

DIY EGG DECORATING

Create an egg-cellent Easter decoration you can hang just about anywhere using a bunch of fun techniques.

Hoppy Easter!

SUPPLIES:

- Cardstock
- Crayola Colored Pencils
- Scrap paper
- Crayola Washable Paint
- Crayola Paintbrushes
- Disposable plate
- Sponge
- Crayola Crayon, white
- Crayola Washable Watercolors
- Water
- Disposable cup
- Crayola Oil Pastels
- Paper clips
- Crayola Construction Paper, brown and green
- Crayola Scissors
- Crayola Glue Stick
- Crayola Metallic Markers

STEPS:

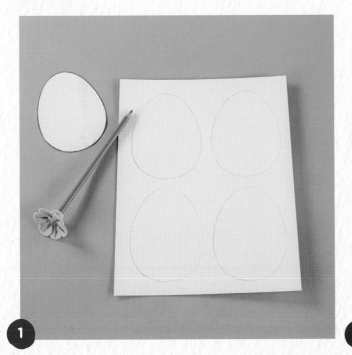

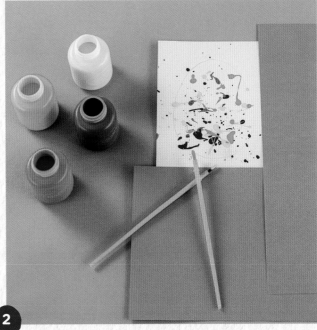

---

1. Draw egg shapes on a piece of cardstock with a colored pencil.

CIY STAFF TIP!
Trace around an egg-shaped cookie cutter to get really eggy-looking eggs.

2. Decorate the egg shapes using a few different techniques. For a paint splatter egg, cover all but one egg with scrap paper. Load a generous amount of washable paint onto two paintbrushes and flick the paint at the cardstock by tapping the paintbrushes together.

3

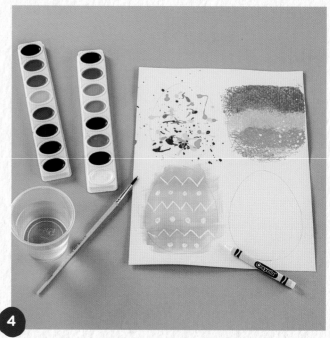

4

5

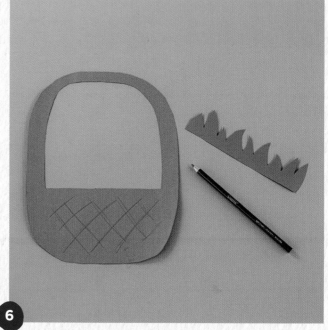

6

3. To make a sponge-paint egg, pour washable paint onto a disposable plate. Dip a sponge into the paint and dab onto the cardstock. Repeat with different colors, filling the egg.

4. To decorate a watercolor reveal egg, draw a design on the egg using a white crayon. Brush washable watercolors over the egg to reveal your design.

5. To create a scratch-art egg, decorate an egg with different color oil pastels. Then color a layer of black oil pastel over the entire egg. Use the rounded edge of a paper clip to scratch a design into the black layer and reveal the color underneath.

6. Draw a basket on brown construction paper and grass on green construction paper. Decorate the basket using colored pencils. Cut out the eggs, basket, and grass with scissors.

7. Using a glue stick, attach the grass and eggs onto the back of the basket.

8. Write a fun Easter message on the basket with metallic markers!

EASTER EGG ORNAMENTS

Create DIY Easter Egg Ornaments out of Crayola Model Magic and hang them around the house or on an Easter tree!

HELP FROM ADULTS
Little crafters may need you to make the hole in their eggs using the paperclip in step 4.

SUPPLIES:

- Crayola Model Magic® Shape 'n Cut Tools
- Crayola Model Magic®
- Egg-shaped cookie cutter
- Paper clip
- Crayola Markers
- Crayola Glitter Glue
- Crayola Scissors
- String

STEPS:

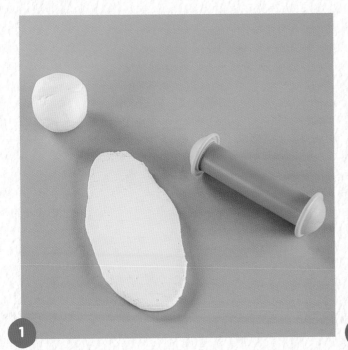

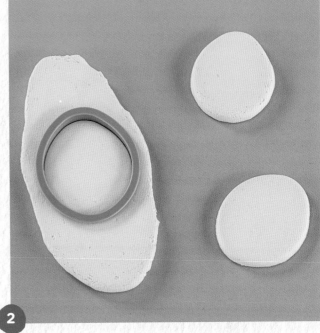

1. Using Shape 'n Cut tools, roll out Crayola Model Magic about ½ inch thick on a smooth, flat surface.

2. Use an egg-shaped cookie cutter to create ornaments from the Crayola Model Magic.

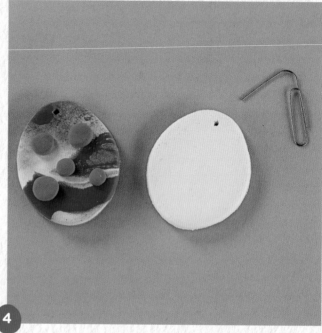

3. Experiment by twisting Crayola Model Magic colors together for a marbleized look or adding small Crayola Model Magic dots to the eggs.

4. Use a partially unfolded paper clip to create a small hole close to the top of the eggs.

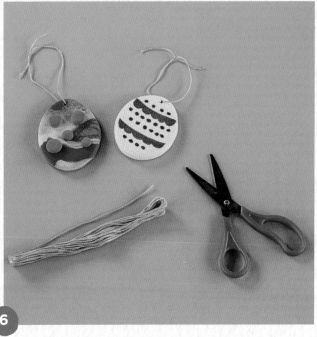

5. Allow the ornaments to dry overnight, and then decorate with markers and glitter glue.

6. Cut a piece of string, loop it through the hole in the ornament, and tie a knot using both ends of the string.

7. Hang your Easter Egg Ornaments around your home or on your Easter tree!

RAINDROP SUNCATCHER

Create a colorful suncatcher using crayon shavings to ring in spring!

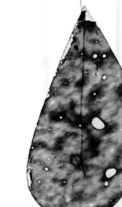

HELP FROM ADULTS

Kids will need help with using the hair dryer in step 5.

SUPPLIES:

- Crayola Crayons
- Crayola Crayon Sharpener
- Wax paper
- Duct tape
- Hair dryer
- Crayola Scissors
- Wooden dowel
- String
- Clear tape

STEPS:

1. Unwrap the crayons in the colors you want to use to make your raindrops.

2. Use the crayon sharpener to create shavings.

CIY STAFF TIP!

A pencil sharpener will work if you don't have a crayon sharpener on hand.

3

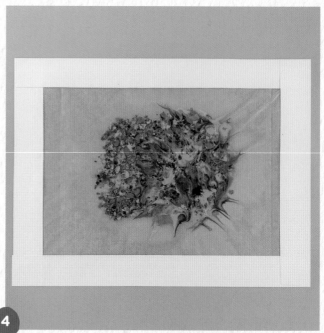

4

5

6

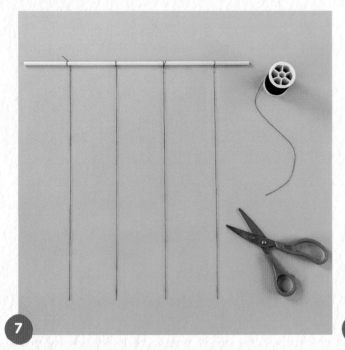

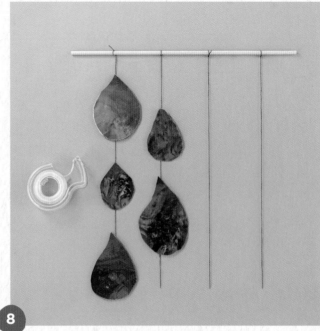

3. Lay a piece of wax paper on a protected surface. Evenly sprinkle the shavings onto the wax paper.

4. Place a slightly larger piece of wax paper over the shavings. Tape down the edges using duct tape.

5. Use a hair dryer to melt the shavings. Let them cool for 15 minutes.

6. Cut out raindrop shapes, leaving the wax paper on.

7. Tie a length of string around the wooden dowel.

8. Tape the raindrops onto the string using clear tape.

9. Repeat with more string and more raindrops. Trim the excess from the end of each string. Enjoy catching a sun shower!

CIY STAFF TIPS!

Experiment with shades of blue for your raindrops.
Tape your raindrops so they hang at different heights.

FLOWER PENCIL TOPPERS

Think spring with Flower Pencil Toppers made from Crayola Model Magic that you can keep in a customized pencil holder—a cute and easy craft to spring into the season with!

CIY STAFF TIP!

When pouring paint onto the flowerpot, alternate colors for a blended effect.

SUPPLIES:

- Crayola Washable Paint
- Disposable cups
- Measuring spoons
- Water
- Craft sticks
- Small terra-cotta flowerpot
- Disposable plate
- Crayola Model Magic®
- Crayola Colored Pencils
- Crayola Glitter Glue

STEPS:

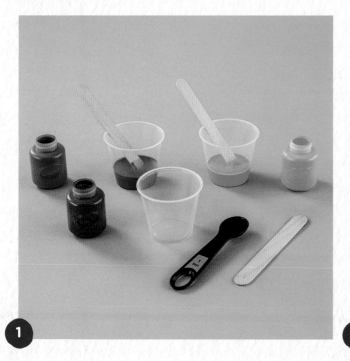

1. First, let's make the pencil holder. Pour paint into a disposable cup and mix with 1 teaspoon of water, stirring with a craft stick until smooth. Repeat with 2 or 3 other colors.

2. Place a disposable cup that is a bit wider than the flowerpot upside down on a disposable plate. Place the flowerpot upside down on top of the cup. Pour the paint mixtures, one by one, over flowerpot, letting the paint drip down the sides. Let the paint dry for 3–4 hours.

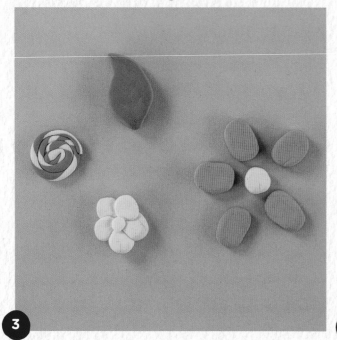

3

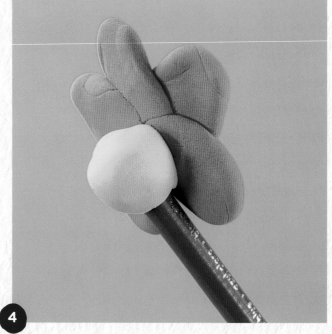

4

---

3. Now, on to the flowers! Create petals, flower middles, and leaves with Crayola Model Magic.

4. Roll a piece of Crayola Model Magic into a ball so that it is approximately 1 inch in diameter. Form the ball around the end of a colored pencil. Press the flowers and leaves against the ball to attach.

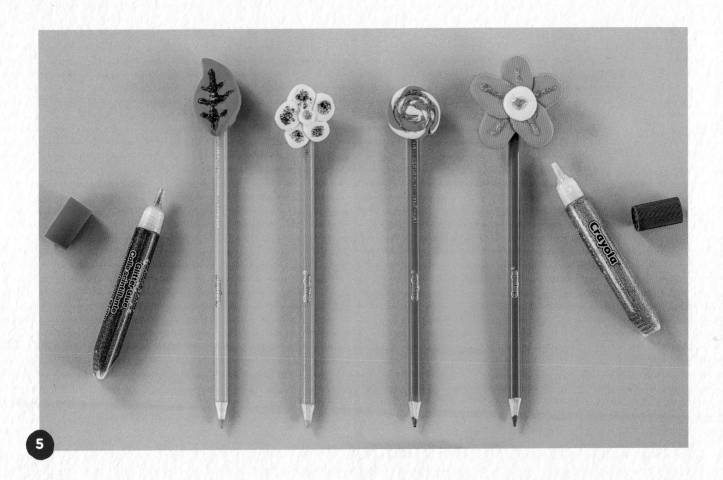

5. Decorate the flowers and leaves with glitter glue details. Let them dry overnight.

6. Place the colored pencils with Flower Pencil Toppers into the pencil holder and display!

CIY STAFF TIPS!

You can make any shape of pencil topper you like! Crayola Model Magic pieces that haven't dried will easily adhere to one another. For added strength, or to attach dried pieces of Crayola Model Magic together, use Crayola Washable No-Run School Glue.

MOTHER'S DAY WREATH

Create a colorful, customizable Mother's Day flower wreath to brighten up Mom's special day!

SUPPLIES:

- Crayola Washable Markers
- Coffee filters
- Water
- Jar or cup
- Paper towels
- Foam wreath
- Burlap or other fabric strip
- Tape
- Chenille stems
- Crayola Scissors
- Decorative leaves

STEPS:

1

2

1. Use the markers to color designs on the coffee filters. Fold each coffee filter in half three times to create a triangle shape. Create enough to make an asymmetrical-looking wreath! We made eight flowers.

2. Put a little water in a jar or cup that has a mouth narrower than the folded coffee filter. Place the folded coffee filter in the jar or cup so that the tip of the triangle touches the water. Watch as the color is wicked up and spreads around! Place the wet coffee filters on paper towels and allow to dry.

CIY STAFF TIP!

You can also create flowers by placing a coffee filter on top of a paper towel, decorating the coffee filter with markers, then painting over the filter with water so the color bleeds through to the paper towel.

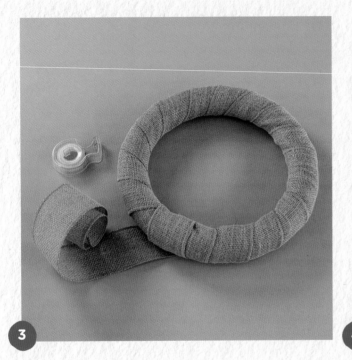

3

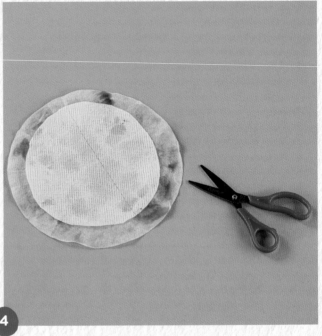

4

3. While the flowers are drying, wrap a foam circle wreath with a fabric of your choice. We used burlap for a country vibe. Tape down the edge of the fabric to start, so that it stays put. Once you've wrapped the entire wreath, tuck the end of the fabric into the layers of wrapped fabric.

4. Cut the paper towels the coffee filters dried on so they are a little smaller than the coffee filters. Place each towel on top of a filter.

CIY STAFF TIP!

Mix and match different colors of paper towel and filters to get a variety of exciting flower designs.

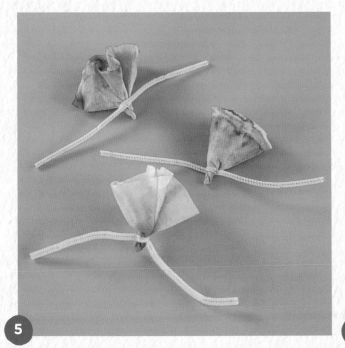

5. Fold each coffee filter and paper towel in half twice, and then twist the bottom from the center to create the shape of a flower. Repeat to create all of the flowers. Wrap the end of each flower with one end of a chenille stem to secure the flower.

6. Wrap the long part of each chenille stem around the wreath and then around the base of the flower to secure it to the wreath. If the flower feels too loose, use a small piece of tape to hold it in place. Add decorative leaves to accent before giving it to Mom!

DECOUPAGE MOTHER'S DAY PICTURE FRAME

Create picture-perfect decoupage art for Mom with this picture frame craft.

SUPPLIES:

- Coloring pages printed for free from Crayola.com
- Crayola Crayons
- Crayola Colored Pencils
- Crayola Scissors
- Crayola Washable No-Run School Glue
- Water
- Measuring cup
- Mason jar
- Craft stick
- Crayola Paintbrush
- Wooden picture frame
- Crayola Acrylic Paint

STEPS:

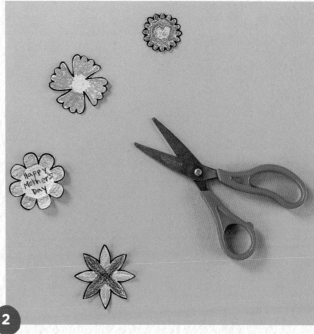

1. Print the free coloring pages and color in the shapes you like with crayons and colored pencils.

2. Cut out the coloring page shapes with scissors and set them aside.

3

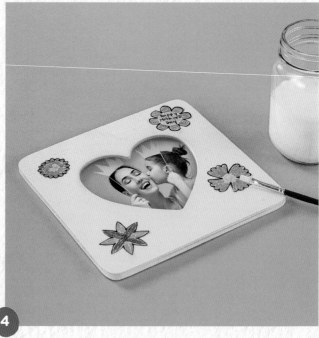

4

3. To make a decoupage mixture, combine ½ cup of of glue and ½ cup of water in a mason jar and mix with a craft stick until fully combined.

4. Flip over the coloring page cutouts and apply the decoupage mixture to the back using a paintbrush. Place them color side up on the picture frame. Brush more decoupage mixture over the images to adhere them to the picture frame.

5. Sign your work and add embellishments using paint.

6. Place a picture in the frame to complete your Mother's Day gift, or let Mom choose a photo of her own.

CIY STAFF TIP! Save any leftover decoupage mixture for future projects!

CIY STAFF TIP!

For an extra personal touch, draw your own piece of art to decoupage to the frame.

DIY SQUISHIES

Easy to make and fun to squeeze, DIY Squishies are a cool craft for kids to create, plus they make great gifts for friends, family, and teachers. You can make all sorts of DIY Squishies—doughnuts, watermelon wedges, animal faces—depending on how you cut and paint the memory foam. Here's how we made our pizza.

HELP FROM ADULTS

Kids may need help cutting the memory foam.

SUPPLIES:

- Memory foam pillow
- Scissors
- Disposable cups
- Measuring spoons
- Water
- Crayola Acrylic Paint (we used brown, red, yellow, and blue to make our pizza)
- Crayola Paintbrushes

STEPS:

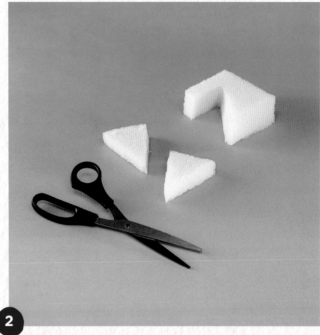

1. Remove the outer cover from the memory foam pillow and cut a small square portion from the corner.

2. Slowly cut away small pieces from the memory foam square to reach your desired shape, such as the triangle slice we used for our pizza.

CIY STAFF TIP!
Budget-friendly memory foam pillows can be found at most big retailers or online.

3. In a disposable cup, mix 1/2 tablespoon of water with 2 tablespoons of brown acrylic paint until fully combined.

4. Paint the top and sides to create the crust.

CIY STAFF TIP!

The paint mixture will be about four parts of paint to one part of water for most colors. It should be smooth but not runny. Add more water in small increments to thin the paint mixture if needed; add more paint to thicken.

6

5. Mix different colors of acrylic paint with water to add toppings like cheese, pepperoni, and peppers! (Blue and yellow mixed together will give you pepper green.) Let the paint dry overnight.

6. Once the paint has dried, squish away! Squish! Squish! Squish!

CIY STAFF TIP!
Save leftover pillow pieces to create more shapes for your DIY Squishy collection.

OMBRE DIP–DYE STRING ART

You can dip-dye string with Crayola Watercolors to create amazing ombre wall art! Mix and match watercolors to form a colorful, bright pattern.

SUPPLIES:

- Ruler
- White string
- Crayola Scissors
- Wooden dowel
- Crayola Watercolors
- Large mixing bowl
- Measuring cup
- Warm water
- Whisk

STEPS:

1. Measure and cut even lengths of white string, enough to fill the length of the wooden dowel.

2. Tie the string around the dowel to create long fringe. Tighten to secure.

CIY STAFF TIP!

Tie the string to the dowel in whatever method you prefer. We used lark's head knots to secure our string, which means we folded the string in half, put the looped end over the dowel, and pulled the two loose ends through the loop.

CIY STAFF TIP!

Once the string has dried, experiment with cutting the strings on an angle for a fun effect.

3. Remove the watercolor tablets from the case. Place 2 or 3 light-colored watercolor tablets into a large mixing bowl.

4. Add 1 ¼ cups of warm water to the bowl and whisk to dissolve the watercolors.

5. Submerge the string into the bowl about ¾ of the way up the string for 30 seconds. Remove the string from the bowl and set it aside on a protected surface.

6. Empty and rinse the bowl and repeat steps 3–5 as many times as you'd like, using progressively darker colors in the same color family and submerging the string at a shallower length each time. Allow the string to dry overnight.

7. Hang to display as wall art!

CIY STAFF TIP!

Mix and match watercolors to create custom colors!

7

SUMMER

Kick off summer fun with a Paper Pinwheel, Father's Day DIY Tic-Tac-Toe, and a hunt for DIY Dinosaur Eggs! Kids won't be sweating these crafts that really beat the heat.

PAPER PINWHEEL

This patterned pinwheel is a summer favorite! Just give it a blow or bring it to the breezy beach and watch it spin round and round.

SUPPLIES:

- Crayola Bright Pop! Cardstock
- Ruler
- Crayola No. 2 Pencil
- Crayola Scissors
- Crayola Ultra-Clean Washable® Stampers
- Hole punch
- Brass fastener
- Paper straw

STEPS:

---

1. Pick your favorite pattern of cardstock.

2. Using the ruler and a pencil, lightly draw a 6-by-6-inch square on the cardstock. Then cut out the square.

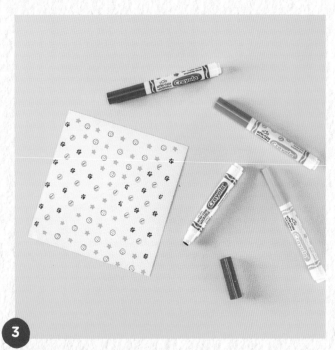

3

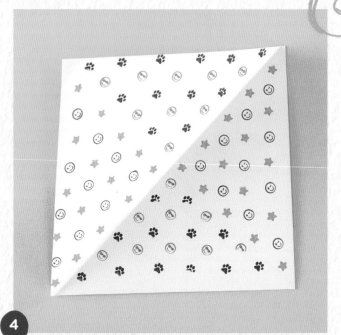

4

5

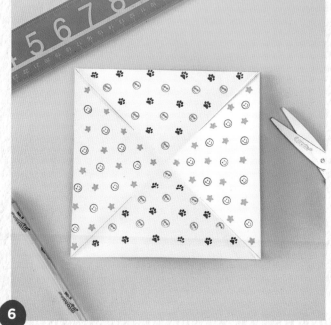

6

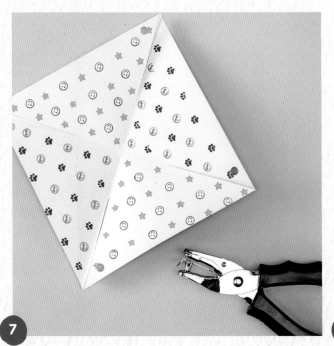

3. Decorate the non-patterned side of the cardstock with the stamper markers.

4. With the stamped side facing up, fold the bottom right corner to the top left corner, creating a triangle. Press along the fold to make a crease. Unfold.

5. Fold the bottom left corner to the top right corner, creating a triangle. Press along the fold to make a crease. Unfold.

6. Using the ruler and a pencil, measure 3 inches from each corner toward the center along the crease and make a light mark. Then cut along each crease, from the corner to the mark.

7. Punch a hole near the corner to the right of the bottom left slit.

8. Rotate the paper and repeat until each side has a hole punched.

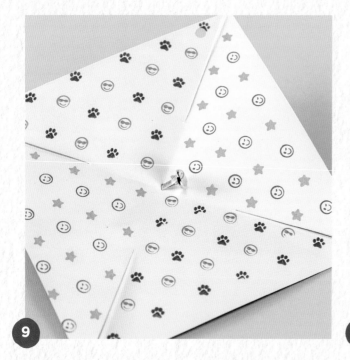

9

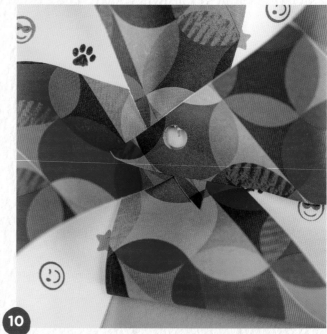

10

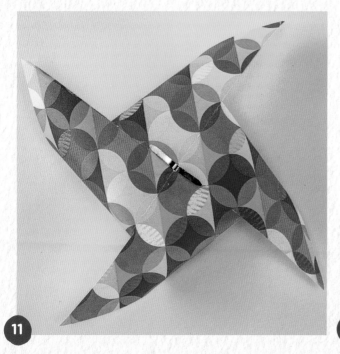

11

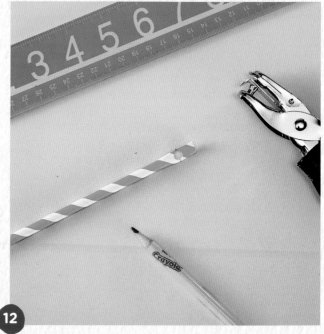

12

13.

14.

9. Use the brass fastener to create a small slit in the center of the cardstock.

10. Fold the corners to the center so the punched holes overlap.

11. Hold the cardstock in place and insert the brass fastener from the front. Flatten the legs of the fastener to hold the pinwheel in place.

12. Flatten the end of the straw and use the ruler to measure 1/2 inch from the end. Mark with the pencil and punch a hole at the mark.

13. Straighten the legs of the fastener and put them through the hole in the straw. Flatten the legs again to finish your pinwheel.

14. Decorate them, or blow into the corners and watch it spin!

CIY STAFF TIP!
Keep the brass fastener a little loose to help the pinwheel spin faster.

FATHER'S DAY DIY TIC-TAC-TOE

Kids can show Dad he rocks by creating this handmade gift that's also a classic game!

YOU ROCK DAD
♥Love, Stephanie

SUPPLIES:

- 10 rocks
- Crayola Acrylic Paint
- Crayola Paintbrushes
- Crayola Fabric Markers
- Canvas bag to hold the rocks
- Crayola Markers
- Paper

STEPS:

1

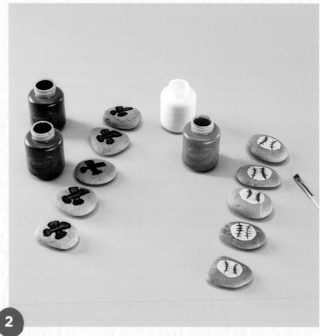

2

1. Divide the 10 rocks into two equal groups.

CIY Staff Tip!

Rocks that are round and somewhat flat are easiest to paint on and make the best game pieces.

2. Using the paint, decorate one group of rocks with a mark or design to symbolize X's and the other group of rocks with a mark or design to symbolize O's. We used crossed bats for our X's and baseballs for our O's. Allow the paint to dry for 1-2 hours.

3

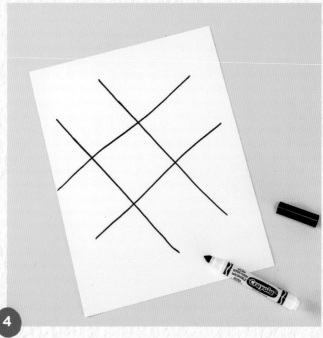

4

3. Using fabric markers, draw, color, and write a personal Father's Day message on the canvas bag.

4. Using markers, create a tic-tac-toe game board on a sheet of paper.

5. Put the rocks in the bag, give the gift to Dad on his special day, and play!

CIY STAFF TIP!

Use Crayola Sidewalk Chalk to make an outdoor tic-tac-toe game board!

5

FATHER'S DAY WOOD PHOTO TRANSFER

Create a photo transfer on wood for a personalized DIY Father's Day gift. Your favorite picture of Dad makes this homemade Father's Day gift extra special!

CIY STAFF TIP!

You can make this thoughtful handmade gift for any special occasion.

SUPPLIES:

- Black-and-white photo with Dad printed on regular paper
- Crayola Paintbrushes
- Crayola Watercolors
- Water
- Disposable cup
- Crayola Scissors
- Crayola Washable No-Run School Glue
- Measuring cup
- Mason jar with lid
- Wood plaque
- Crayola Super Tips Washable Markers

STEPS:

1. On the printed black-and-white photo, use the paintbrushes to add watercolor in areas you want to highlight. Allow the paint to dry for 1–2 hours.

2. Cut out the image with scissors. Set aside.

3

4

3. Create a glue mixture by pouring ½ cup of glue and ½ cup of water into a mason jar. Twist on the lid and shake until well combined.

4. Apply the glue mixture to the back of the photo using a paintbrush. Place the photo on the plaque. Apply some additional glue mixture with the brush to the front of the photo to seal the edges.

CIY STAFF TIP!

A glossy photograph will not work for this project.

5

6

5. Paint supporting designs with water on the plaque, then fill in the water designs with watercolors. Allow the paint to dry for 1–2 hours.

6. Write a thoughtful message for Dad and sign the plaque using the markers.

7. Give the finished wood plaque to Dad on Father's Day!

ROCK ART ANIMALS

Whether at camp or in the backyard, turning found rocks into Rock Art Animals is a fun and colorful summer craft that combines rock painting and Crayola Model Magic.

CIY STAFF TIP!

You can make a variety of other animals, including a bird or a rabbit!

SUPPLIES:

- Rocks
- Crayola Acrylic Paint
- Disposable plate
- Craft sticks
- Crayola Paintbrush
- Crayola Model Magic®
- Crayola Washable No-Run School Glue
- Crayola Metallic Markers

STEPS:

1

2

1. Pick a small rock from outside for each animal you want to make. We made a snail and a turtle. Wash the rocks and allow them to dry, if needed.

2. Mix paint on the disposable plate with a craft stick to get the colors of your choice. We mixed white and red for our pink snail shell and blue and yellow paint to get a green turtle shell.

CIY STAFF TIP!

For added sheen, mix pearlescent medium into the paint.

3

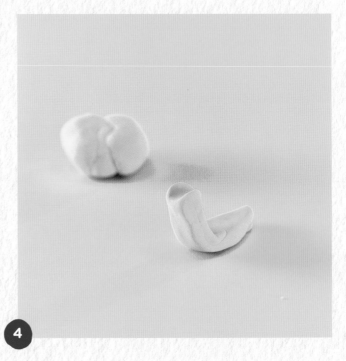

4

3. Paint the rock, then allow it to dry for 1 hour. Apply a second coat of paint and allow to dry for 1–2 hours.

4. Shape Crayola Model Magic into the body or parts of the animal you need. We started with the snail's body.

5. Then glue the rock onto the Crayola Model Magic.

6. Add accents and a face using the metallic markers.

7

8

7. To create our turtle, first we painted the top of the rock to be the turtle's shell. Then we shaped the head, legs, and tail out of Crayola Model Magic.

8. Then we glued the head, legs, and tail to the bottom of the rock.

9

10

9. We also shaped Crayola Model Magic into the shell details and glued them to the top of the rock.

10. Then we added a face with markers.

11. Allow the glue and Crayola Model Magic to dry overnight, then take the animals out to play or put them on display!

DIY TERRARIUM

A homemade terrarium coming right up! Let sunny weather inspire this kids' terrarium that brings a little bit of nature indoors, complete with a ladybug made from air-dry clay.

SUPPLIES:

- Crayola Air-Dry Clay
- Chenille stems
- Crayola Acrylic Paint
- Crayola Paintbrush
- Crayola Glitter Glue
- Crayola Scissors
- Crayola Window Crayons
- Crayola Window Markers
- Glass bowl
- Soil

CIY STAFF TIP!
Make a smaller version of this terrarium using a mason jar.

STEPS:

1

2

---

1. To make the ladybug for inside the terrarium, roll one large and one medium ball of clay. Push them together to connect the body and head. Roll two small balls of clay for the eyes, then push them onto the head (the medium ball), flattening them a bit.

2. Using a chenille stem, poke two holes in the head behind the eyes, then remove the chenille stems. This is where the antennae will go. Allow the ladybug body to dry overnight.

CIY STAFF TIP!

Want a different theme? Create a different animal out of Crayola Model Magic or Crayola Air-Dry Clay and draw a corresponding scene on the outside of the bowl.

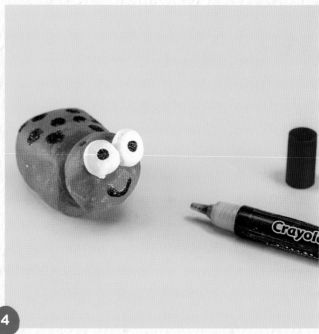

7

8

3. Paint the body and head red using a paintbrush. Allow the paint to dry for 1–2 hours.

4. Using blue glitter glue, add spots to the ladybug's body. Put one small dot on each of the eyes. Allow the glue to dry for 3–4 hours.

5. Cut a chenille stem in half (or smaller) for the antennae. Insert one piece into each of the poked holes. Curl and shape as desired.

6. Use window crayons and window markers to draw a nature scene on the outside of the bowl.

7. Fill the bottom of the bowl with soil, then place your ladybug inside.

8. Display your terrarium anywhere in the house where you want to bring a little sunshine inside.

CIY STAFF TIP!

You can use all sorts of found objects and earthy elements in your terrarium.

JULY FOURTH DECORATIONS

Resist art is magically revealed by drawing patterns and designs in white crayon and then painting over them with vibrant watercolors, which exposes the seemingly hidden white crayon resist designs. It's a little bit of craft magic kids love! Celebrate Independence Day with DIY sparklers and watercolor resist flag decorations! They make wonderful additions to your July Fourth party décor.

SUPPLIES:

- Crayola Crayons
- Cardstock, white and black
- Crayola Watercolors
- Water
- Disposable cup
- Crayola Paintbrush
- Bamboo skewers
- Clear tape
- Crayola Washable No-Run School Glue
- Salt
- Crayola Glitter Glue
- Crayola Scissors

CRAYON RESIST FLAG STEPS:

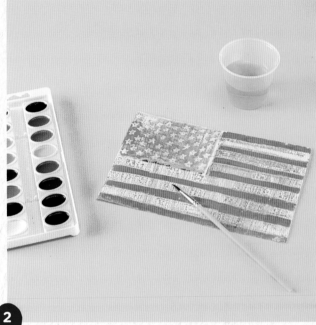

1. Draw stars and stripes with a white crayon on a rectangular piece of white cardstock, coloring in the white stripes of the flag.

2. Paint over the crayon with red and blue watercolors to reveal the resist. Allow the paint to dry for 1–2 hours.

3. Tape a bamboo skewer to the dried flag.

STEPS:

1

2

1. Draw fireworks on black cardstock using school glue. Then sprinkle your drawing with salt. Tilt cardstock and lightly shake off excess salt.

2. Lightly dab watercolor paint onto the salt and glue, letting it spread. Allow it to dry for 1–2 hours.

CIY STAFF TIP!

Experiment with different shades of watercolors and glitter glue to make your sparklers.

3. Now draw fireworks with glitter glue on a new sheet of black cardstock. Allow them to dry for 3–4 hours.

4. Cut out the firework shapes and tape a bamboo skewer to each cutout.

5. Arrange a firework display with the flag as a festive centerpiece!

CIY STAFF TIP!
You can hand out the DIY sparklers as a safer alternative to traditional sparklers!

DIY DINOSAUR EGGS

Play like a paleontologist by making and breaking open your own dinosaur eggs! They are perfect to trade with friends, give out as party favors, or hide around the yard for a dino egg hunt.

CIY STAFF TIP!

Experiment with placing other small hidden treasures inside your eggs for endless surprises!

SUPPLIES:

- Crayola Air-Dry Clay, white
- Small dinosaur toys
- Disposable plate
- Crayola Washable Paint
- Crayola Paintbrush

STEPS:

1. Flatten out a section of clay big enough to wrap around a small dinosaur toy.

2. Leaving a space to create a hollow center, fold the clay around the dinosaur and mold the clay to create an egg shape. Repeat for additional eggs. Allow them to dry overnight.

3. On a disposable plate, paint the eggs to give them some color. Allow the paint to dry for 1–2 hours.

4. Trade the dino eggs with friends! Break them open using the end of a paintbrush to see what's inside.

AIR–DRY CLAY IMPRINTS

Preserve summer memories (or any special moment!) by making air-dry clay keepsakes you can put on display. Imprint found objects, then make the clay impressions pop with paint!

SUPPLIES:

- Wax paper
- Crayola Air-Dry Clay, white
- Rolling pin
- Found objects, for example, seashells, ferns, flowers, or leaves
- Crayola Paintbrushes
- Crayola Washable Paint

STEPS:

1. On wax paper, flatten a large clay ball with a rolling pin to create a surface for your imprints. Make it thick enough to hold your impressions! About $\frac{1}{2}$–1 inch should do it.

2. Press the found objects into the flattened clay to make imprints. For hard objects like shells, you can wobble them around to get all the details. For soft objects like plants, press them into the clay and leave them there. Dry the clay overnight.

3. Remove any found objects you left in the clay.

4. Allow the paint to dry for 1–2 hours, then display!

CIY STAFF TIP!
You can also experiment decorating with Crayola Watercolors.

COLORFUL HAND FAN

Keep cool on hot summer days with a custom hand fan. You can personalize them with your favorite fruit or a colorful pattern!

HELP FROM ADULTS

Kids will need an adult to poke holes into the craft sticks.

SUPPLIES:

- 4 craft sticks
- Cardstock
- Crayola No. 2 Pencil
- Crayola Watercolors
- Water
- Disposable cup
- Crayola Paintbrush
- Crayola Washable Paint
- Crayola Super Tips Washable Markers
- Crayola Glitter Glue
- Crayola Scissors
- Brass fastener
- Crayola Washable No-Run School Glue

STEPS:

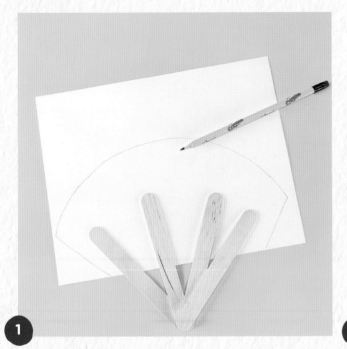

1

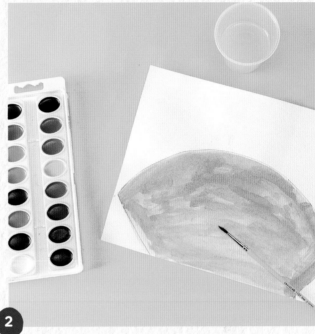

2

---

1. Fan out four craft sticks on the cardstock as a guide for the size and shape of the fan. Using a pencil, outline the arched shape of a fan.

2. With the watercolors, paint a design within the arched shape. Allow the paint to dry for 1–2 hours.

CIY STAFF TIP!
Experiment with different watercolor designs to customize your fan!

DIY PUFFY PAINT ICE CREAM

An easy summer craft is a few scoops away! Make DIY puffy paint and use it as part of this ice cream craft you can create and hang.

SUPPLIES:

- Corrugated cardboard
- Crayola Scissors
- Crayola Washable No-Run School Glue
- Cardstock
- Measuring cups
- Foaming shaving cream
- 2 disposable cups
- Craft sticks
- Crayola Washable Paint
- Crayola Paintbrush
- Crayola Construction Paper, red and brown
- Crayola Crayon Sharpener
- Crayola Crayons

STEPS:

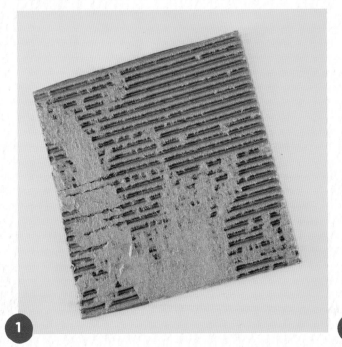

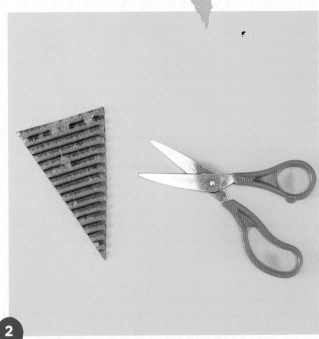

1

2

1. Rip the top layer off a small piece of corrugated cardboard to create the texture of an ice cream cone.

2. Cut the cardboard into a cone shape with the scissors.

CIY STAFF TIP!

For really puffy ice cream, build up the glue mixture when applying it to the cardstock.

3

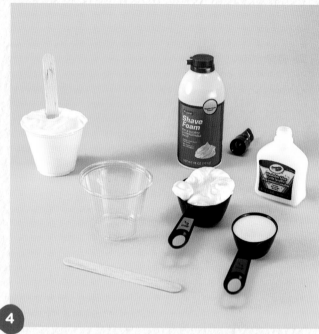

4

5

6

3. Put glue on the smooth side of the cardboard and attach it to the cardstock.

4. Mix ½ cup of shaving cream and 1/4 cup of glue with a craft stick in each cup, giving you two glue mixture puffy paint bases.

5. Lightly dip a clean craft stick into a pot of washable paint, and then use it to stir the glue mixture. Repeat with another color and the other cup of glue mixture.

6. Paint each colored glue mixture above the ice cream cone, making two ice cream scoops.

7. Cut out a cherry shape from red construction paper and triangle chips and a cherry stem from brown construction paper and place them on the glue mixture.

8. Use the sharpener to create crayon shavings. Sprinkle them onto the glue mixture to create sprinkles. Allow your puffy painting to dry overnight.

9. Once dry, enjoy the fun, fluffy feeling and hang to display!

CIY STAFF TIP!

The Crayola 120-count Crayon box includes a crayon sharpener.

UPCYCLED STORAGE JAR

Organize craft supplies inside a cool, upcycled DIY storage jar. The Crayola Model Magic topper on the lid makes this kids' craft fun to make and display!

ADULT SUPERVISION REQUIRED

SUPPLIES:

- Craft stick
- Crayola Acrylic Paint
- Disposable cup
- Jar with lid
- Crayola Paint Brushes
- Crayola Model Magic®
- Crayola Markers
- Crayola Washable No-Run School Glue

STEPS:

1. With a craft stick, mix together the paint in a disposable cup to create the color you want for the jar lid. We mixed white, yellow, and blue acrylic paint to make a green lid for our monster topper.

2. Remove the lid from the jar, and paint the lid. Allow it to dry for 1–2 hours, then paint a second coat. Allow that to dry for another 1–2 hours.

CIY STAFF TIP!
Make multiple storage jars with other Crayola Model Magic critters on top—the options are endless!

3. Use Crayola Model Magic to make the monster, animal, or critter topper for the lid. Allow it to dry overnight.

4. Use markers to add embellishments to the Crayola Model Magic topper.

5

6

5. Attach the topper to the top of the lid using school glue. Allow the glue to dry for 2 hours.

6. Fill the jar with crayons, craft supplies, paper clips, or anything else on hand!

CIY STAFF TIP!

Use Crayola Glitter Glue to add shimmery accents to the Crayola Model Magic.

PENNY PAPER SPINNERS

Put your lucky penny to good use in a colorful paper spinner! This fun DIY fidget toy comes in handy on long trips and slow summer days.

HELP FROM ADULTS

Kids will need an adult to cut the slit into the spinner using a craft knife in step 7 and to hot glue the penny in place in step 9.

SUPPLIES:

- Crayola No. 2 Pencil
- Disposable cup
- Crayola Construction Paper
- Crayola Scissors
- Crayola Colored Pencils
- Crayola Markers
- Thin scrap cardboard (like an old clothing gift box or cereal box)
- Crayola Washable No-Run School Glue
- Craft knife
- Penny
- Hot glue gun and glue

STEPS:

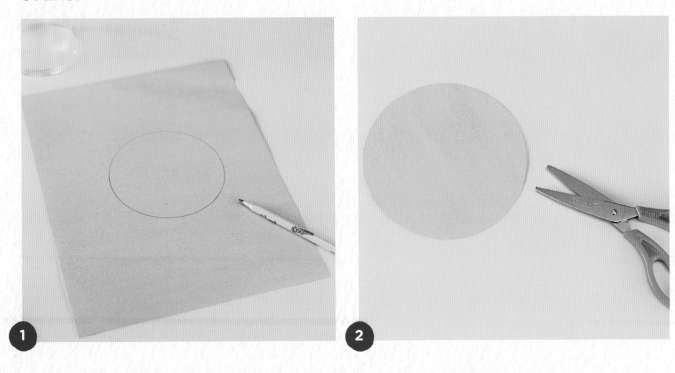

1. Using a pencil, trace the rim of the disposable cup onto the construction paper.

2. Cut out the circle with the scissors.

3

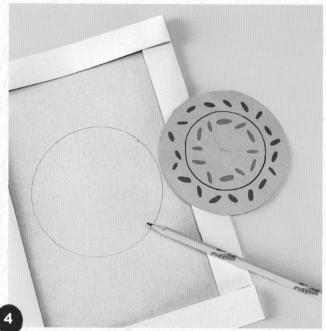

4

6

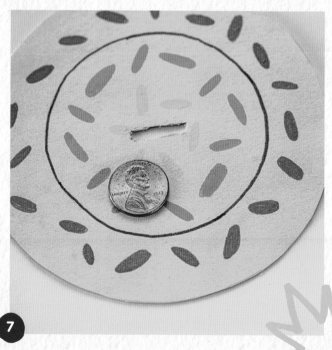

7

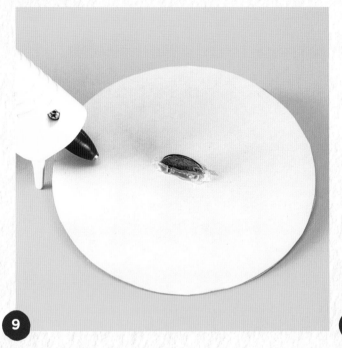

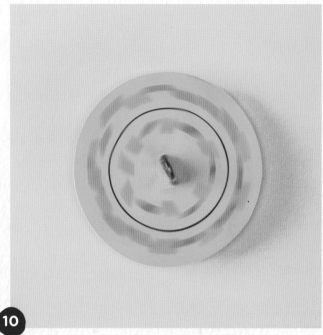

9

10

3. Create designs on the circle with colored pencils and markers.

4. Trace the circle onto a piece of thin cardboard.

5. Cut out the circle with the scissors.

6. Glue the designed circle onto the cardboard circle. Allow the glue to dry for 1–2 hours.

7. Cut a small slit, about the length of a penny, into the center of the disc with craft knife.

8. Lightly push the penny into slit, leaving an equal amount of the penny exposed on the top and the bottom.

9. Secure the penny to the bottom of the cardboard using a hot glue gun.

10. Spin, spin, spin!

CIY STAFF TIP!

Experiment with different patterns to create mesmerizing effects!

FABRIC PATCHES

These custom iron-on patches add a personal touch to your gear! Make them for backpacks, clothing, and other accessories.

HELP FROM ADULTS

Adults will need to iron the patches onto the backpacks, clothing, or accessories in step 4.

CIY STAFF TIP

Customize jeans, canvas sneakers, pencil bags, and more with DIY patches!

SUPPLIES:

- Iron-on fabric patch sheet
- Crayola Fabric Markers
- Crayola Permanent Markers
- Crayola Scissors
- Backpack, clothing, or accessories
- Ironing board
- Iron

STEPS:

1. Draw and color a vibrant design on the iron-on patch sheet using fabric markers and permanent markers.

2. Cut out the patch design.

3. Place the backpack, clothing, or accessory onto an ironing board, and position the patch where you'd like it to go.

4. Iron on the patch to set the color and adhere the patch to the material.

5. Wear here, there, and everywhere!

FALL

Fall is an exciting time of year, with a new school year starting, the leaves changing, and Halloween and Thanksgiving to celebrate. Make your autumn awesome with First Day of School Signs, Haunted Halloween Decorations, and a Turkey Bowling Game!

FIRST DAY OF SCHOOL SIGNS

Make the first day of school even more memorable with a DIY back-to-school sign that can be used from year to year by all the kids in your family!

SUPPLIES:

- Printout of Crayola First Day of School Coloring Page from Crayola.com
- Crayola Colored Pencils
- Picture frame with glass
- Crayola Window Markers
- Paper towels

STEPS:

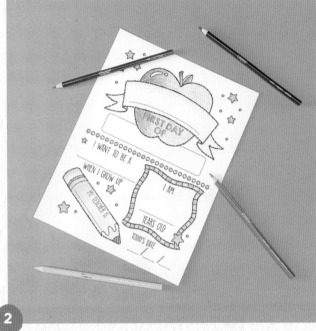

1. Go to Crayola.com and go to the tutorial for this craft, or click on the Coloring & Crafts tab and search for "school." Print the "Apple First Day of School Sign" or "First Day of School Sign" coloring page from Crayola.com. We used the apple sign.

2. Color the page with colored pencils. Trim the page to fit the frame if needed.

CIY STAFF TIP!

Printing the coloring page on a standard piece of 8½-by-11-inch printer paper and trimming it to fit an 8-by-10-inch frame works best, but feel free to experiment by printing larger or smaller.

4

5

3. Remove the back from the picture frame, place the coloring page inside, and reassemble the frame.

4. Fill in the information on the glass pane using window markers.

5. Have your parent take a picture of you holding the frame to create a precious memory!

6. Wipe the frame clean with paper towels to reuse it for another young scholar or for next year.

CIY STAFF TIP!

Crayola Take Note! Dry-Erase Markers will also work in lieu of window markers.

UNI-CREATURES® PENCIL TOPPERS

Be inspired by our Uni-Creatures collection and create unicorn-inspired pencil toppers using Crayola Model Magic. A   sparkly pencil holder is the perfect stable   to store them!

SUPPLIES:

- Crayola Model Magic®
- Crayola Colored Pencils
- Wiggle eyes
- Mason or upcycled jar
- Crayola Washable Glitter Paint
- Crayola Paintbrushes

ADULT SUPERVISION REQUIRED

STEPS:

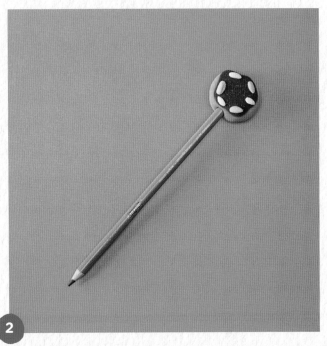

1. To make a topper, roll a 1-inch piece of Crayola Model Magic into a ball, then sculpt it into whatever shape you like for your Uni-Creature's body. Here we pressed it into a disk for a donut Uni-Creature.

2. Use the pointed end of a colored pencil to create a hole in the bottom the topper, then secure the ball on the flat end of the colored pencil.

CIY STAFF TIP!

Using Crayola Model Magic Shimmer Colors will add even more glitter to your Uni-Creatures.

3

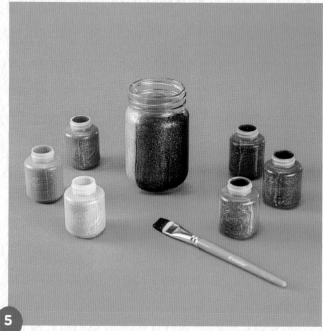

5

---

3. Sculpt unicorn creature features (like a horn!) in different Crayola Model Magic colors and press them onto the topper.

4. Press on the wiggle eyes.

5. To make the sparkly pencil holder, paint a jar in a rainbow pattern using glitter paint. Let the paint dry for 1–2 hours.

6. Store finished pencil toppers in the jar!

CIY STAFF TIP!
Crayola Model Magic that is fresh from the pack will stick to itself. Dried pieces can be glued together.

MODEL MAGIC® DIY BOOKMARKS

Make whimsical bookmarks using paper clips and Crayola Model Magic!

SUPPLIES:

- Crayola Model Magic®
- Jumbo paper clips
- Crayola Markers
- Crayola Glitter Glue

STEPS:

1

3

1. Shape Crayola Model Magic into your favorite animals, flowers, sports balls, or anything else you can imagine.

2. Insert the single-loop end of a jumbo paper clip into the bottom of your shape, being sure to stop before it covers the cut ends of the wire. Let the Crayola Model Magic dry overnight.

3. Decorate your Crayola Model Magic shapes using markers and glitter glue.

4. Use your creations to mark your spot in your favorite book!

CIY Staff Tip!

Experiment mixing and blending two or more colors of Crayola Model Magic to make a marbleized effect or even a new color.

HEART THUMBPRINT ART

Make your parents or Grandma and Grandpa a gift that will warm their hearts!

Cassie Joel Katie Steph Liam Dawn

CIY STAFF TIP!

This is a great activity to do when all the cousins are together and then give as a gift to grandparents on Grandparents Day, the first Sunday after Labor Day.

SUPPLIES:

- Crayola Construction Paper
- Crayola Scissors
- Crayola Creativity Canvas
- Crayola Metallic Markers
- Crayola Washable Paint

STEPS:

1. Create a paper heart shape template using construction paper and scissors. Trace the heart onto the canvas board using a marker.

2. Select a color of Crayola Washable Paint for each person who will be adding their thumbprints to the art.

3. One at a time, have each person dip their thumbs in their color of paint and add their thumbprints inside the traced heart. Have each person add one last thumbprint to the bottom of the picture.

4. Using the markers, write each person's name below their thumbprint at the bottom of the picture to create a colorful legend.

5. Allow your artwork to dry and then display it!

DIY CHALKBOARD PAINT

Create your own chalkboard paint! Use Crayola Acrylic Paints to create your own colorful chalkboard canvas on wooden plaques, coasters, and more.

CIY STAFF TIP!

Chalkboards don't need to be black! You can make yours any color you like.

SUPPLIES:

- Mixing bowl
- Measuring spoons and cups
- 2 tablespoons baking soda
- Water
- Craft stick
- ¼ cup Crayola Acrylic Paint
- Crayola Paintbrush
- Wood plaque, coaster, or other smooth, flat surface
- Crayola Chalk

STEPS:

1. In a mixing bowl, combine 2 tablespoons of baking soda and 1 tablespoon of water and use a craft stick to mix completely, creating a paste.

2. Pour ¼ cup of acrylic paint into the bowl with the baking soda mixture. Stir with a craft stick to combine.

3. Paint the acrylic paint and baking soda mixture onto a smooth, flat object that will be your chalkboard area. Allow to dry completely overnight.

4. Write a message with chalk and display! Wipe away and draw again as often as you like.

WITCH'S CAULDRON

This spooky, glowing brew makes a great window decoration for the Halloween season.

HELP FROM ADULTS

Kids will need help using the hair dryer in step 4.

SUPPLIES:

- Crayola Crayons
- Crayola Crayon Sharpener
- Wax paper
- Duct tape
- Hair dryer
- Crayola No. 2 Pencil
- Crayola Construction Paper
- Crayola Scissors
- Clear tape

STEPS:

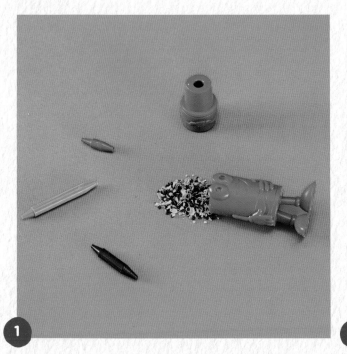

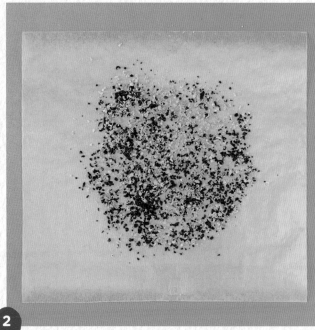

1. Shave three different colored crayons in the crayon sharpener. You'll need enough shavings to fill a small piece of wax paper.

2. Lay a piece of wax paper on a protected surface. Evenly sprinkle the shavings onto the wax paper.

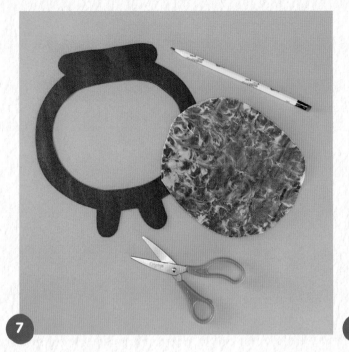

7

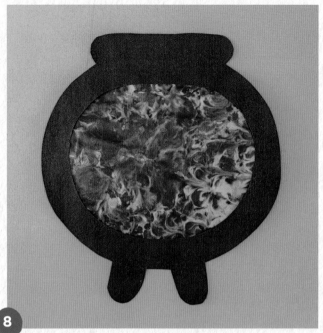

8

3. Place a slightly larger piece of wax paper over the shavings and seal the edges with duct tape.

4. Use a hair dryer to melt the shavings. Let them cool for 15 minutes.

5. Meanwhile, use the pencil to draw a cauldron shape onto construction paper, then draw a large circle in the bowl of the cauldron.

6. Cut out the cauldron shape and the circle in the bowl with scissors.

7. Trace the cauldron onto the cooled wax paper and melted crayon shavings and cut out the shape with scissors.

8. Tape the wax paper and shavings to the back of the cauldron and hang in the window so when the sun shines through, you see an eerie glow!

CIY STAFF TIP!

Experiment making your cauldron brew in whatever spooky colors you like!

HANDPRINT HALLOWEEN CARD

Get your hands dirty creating spooktacular, personalized Halloween greeting cards for friends and family!

SUPPLIES:

- Crayola Construction Paper
- Crayola Paintbrushes
- Crayola Washable Paint
- Crayola No. 2 Pencil
- Crayola Scissors
- Crayola Washable No-Run School Glue
- Wiggle eyes
- Crayola Glitter Markers
- Crayola Super Tips Washable Markers

CIY STAFF TIP!

Use white paint on little kids' feet to make ghoulish ghost versions of this card.

STEPS:

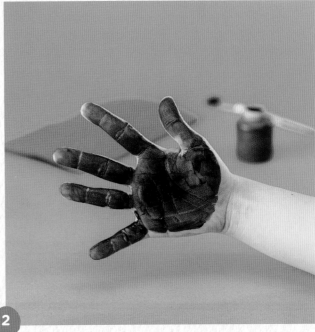

1. Fold a sheet of construction paper in half to create a card.

2. Paint your hand using a paintbrush and black washable paint.

CIY STAFF TIP!

Press down on the child's hand in step 3 to give the kitty's body more shape.

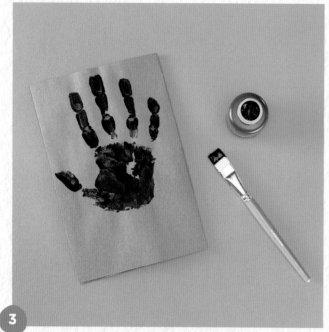

3

4

5

7

9

3. Press your painted hand down onto the front of the construction paper card to create the body of a creepy kitty. Go wash your painted hand! Let the paint on the card dry completely.

4. Using the pencil, draw shapes on construction paper. Make a circle and two triangles for the kitty's head and ears. Create other shapes to decorate the scene. We made a moon and stars. Cut out the shapes.

5. Attach the construction paper shapes to the card using glue.

6. Attach wiggle eyes to the cat's head using glue.

7. Decorate your kitty and card using glitter markers. Write a Halloween greeting.

8. Highlight the details using Super Tips markers.

9. Give the cards to your friends and family.

SUGAR SKULLS

Sculpt colorful sugar skulls out of Crayola Model Magic to decorate your desk or windowsill! A little glitter glue will make them extra festive.

SUPPLIES:

- Crayola Model Magic®
- Crayola Paintbrush
- Crayola Markers
- Crayola Glitter Glue

STEPS:

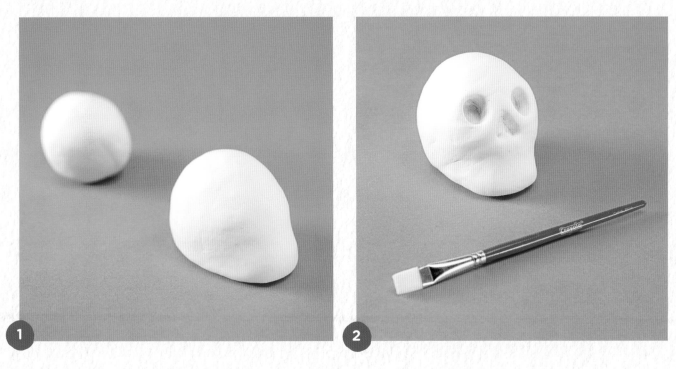

1. Form a large ball of white Crayola Model Magic, about the size of your fist. Sculpt it so it's a little bulbous, like a skull.

2. With your fingers or the end of a paintbrush, press into the clay to create nose holes and eye sockets.

3. Blend in the edges with your fingers and shape until a skull shape is formed. Allow the skull to dry overnight.

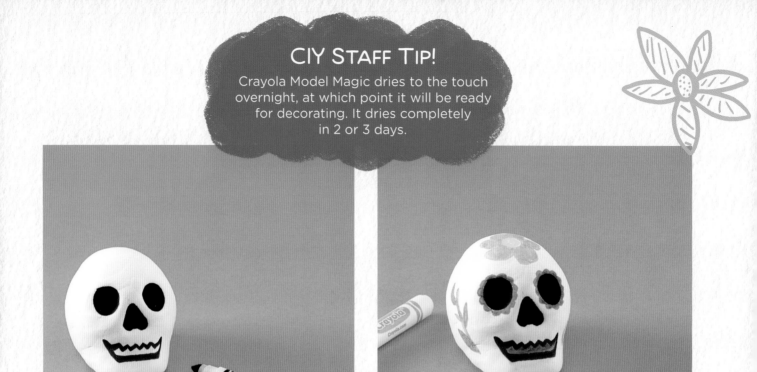

CIY STAFF TIP!

Crayola Model Magic dries to the touch overnight, at which point it will be ready for decorating. It dries completely in 2 or 3 days.

4. Use a black marker to color in the eye sockets and nose holes, and draw an outline for teeth.

5. Draw decorations on your skull using different color markers.

6. Add embellishments such as dots and swirls using glitter glue, and display your sugar skull where everyone can see how sweet it is!

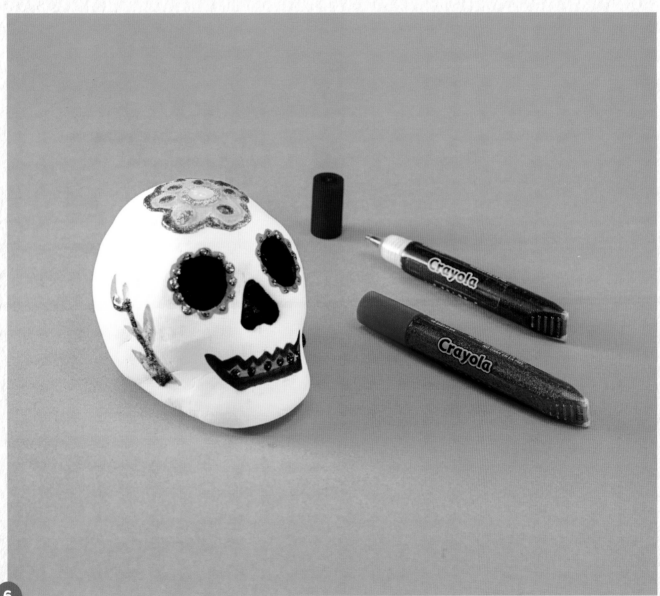

6

HAUNTED HALLOWEEN DECORATIONS

Upcycle empty paper towel rolls into spook-tacular spirits, scary spiders, and other dastardly DIY Halloween decorations. We chose to make a boo-tiful bat below.

HELP FROM ADULTS

Younger crafters may need help cutting into the paper towel tube in steps 1 and 6.

SUPPLIES:

- Paper towel tube
- Crayola Scissors
- Crayola Washable Paint
- Crayola Paintbrush
- Crayola Construction Paper
- Clear tape
- Crayola Washable No-Run School Glue
- Wiggle eyes
- Crayola Metallic Markers

• STEPS:

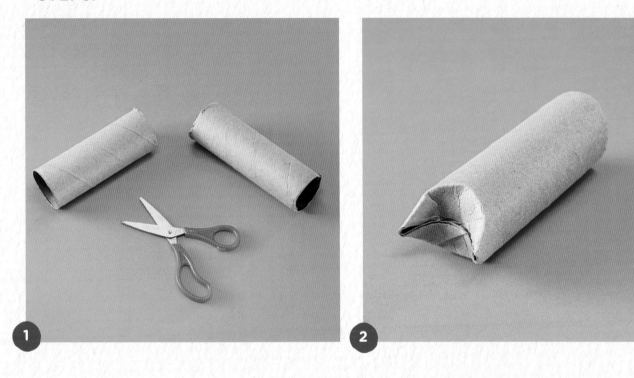

---

1. Cut the paper towel tube in half.

2. On one end, fold both sides of the roll inward to create bat ears.

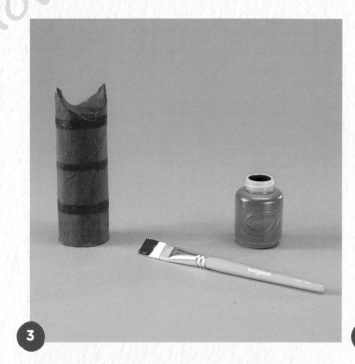

3

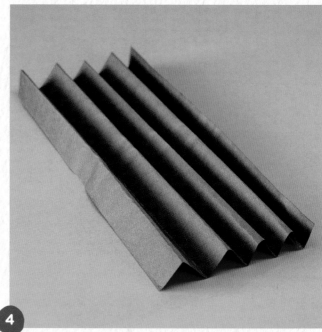

4

5

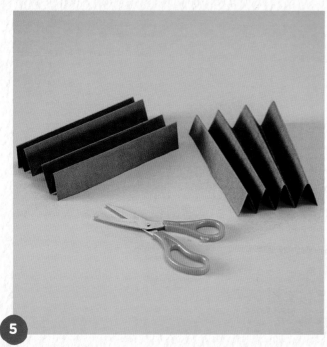

6

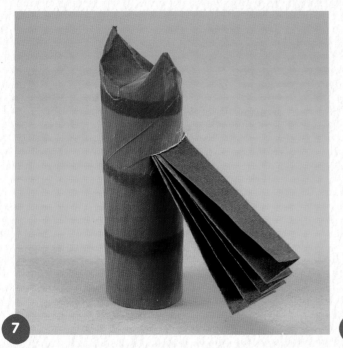

7

8

3. Paint the tube, and allow the paint to dry for 1–2 hours.

4. Accordion-fold a piece of construction paper.

5. Cut the folded construction paper in half.

6. Cut a small slit into the side of the tube.

7. Pinch one end of the construction paper to flatten it, and insert it into the slit.

8. Fan out the construction paper out. Tape the bottom edge of the construction paper to the tube to create a bat wing.

CIY
STAFF TIP!
You can also use wrapping paper tubes.

9

10

9. Repeat steps 6–8 to make a second wing.

10. Glue the wiggle eyes to the roll.

11. Add a mouth and fangs with a marker.

12. Create other creatures and display your decorations.

LEAF STAMP CANVAS

Paint and press fall leaves to create this colorful Thanksgiving print!

GIVE thanks

SUPPLIES:

- Fallen or faux leaves
- Crayola Washable Paint
- Disposable plate
- Crayola Creativity Canvas
- Crayola Paint Brushes

STEPS:

1. Gather fallen or faux leaves of different sizes and shapes.

2. Paint a colorful Thanksgiving message, such as "Give Thanks," in the middle of a canvas using Crayola Washable Paint. Set aside to dry, about 1–2 hours.

3. Pour different colors of paint onto a disposable plate to create your paint palette.

4. Carefully paint one side of a leaf, covering it completely.

5. Press the painted side of the leaf firmly on the edge of the canvas. It's okay if the entire leaf doesn't fit on the canvas.

6. Gently lift up the leaf to reveal the imprint of the painted leaf.

7. Repeat in a variety of colors to fill the border of the canvas and create a beautiful, festive painting! Allow to dry completely, and hang in your home.

6

BLACK GLUE GALAXY PAINTING

Turn a picture frame into galaxy art with homemade black glue and Crayola Watercolors. Have fun painting the galaxy, and then let the light shine through!

HELP FROM ADULTS

Kids will need help removing the glass, placing it on their drawing, and hot gluing it into the frame (steps 4 and 8).

SUPPLIES:

- Measuring spoons
- 2 tablespoons Crayola Washable No-Run School Glue
- Squeeze bottle
- Craft stick
- 1 tablespoon Crayola Acrylic Paint, black
- Cardstock
- Crayola No. 2 Pencil
- Picture frame with plastic or glass pane
- Crayola Watercolors
- Crayola Paintbrush
- Water
- Disposable cup
- Crayola Glitter Glue
- Hot glue gun and glue

STEPS:

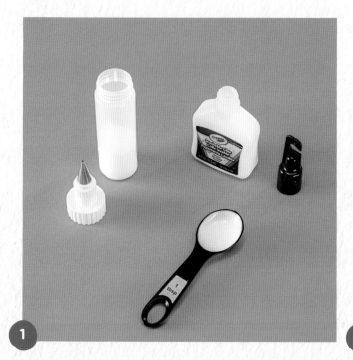

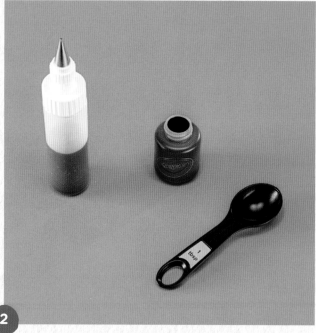

1. Pour the 2 tablespoons of glue into the squeeze bottle.

2. Using a craft stick, mix 1 tablespoon of black paint into the glue. Screw the cap onto the bottle.

CIY Staff Tip!

The amount of glue and paint you need doesn't have to be exactly measured out. As long as you use about two parts of glue to one part of paint, you can eyeball the amounts.

3

5

6

7

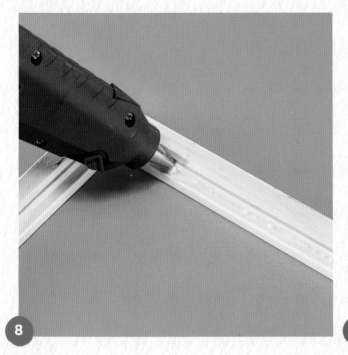

8

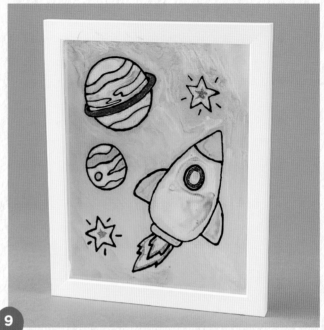

9

3. On a piece of cardstock, draw an outer-space scene with a pencil.

4. Carefully remove the pane from the picture frame and place it on top of the cardstock drawing.

5. Trace the outlines of the drawing onto the pane with the glue mixture. Allow the glue to dry, about 1–2 hours.

6. Paint inside the black-glue outlines using watercolors.

7. Add accents with glitter glue. Allow the painting to dry for 3–4 hours.

8. Attach the edges of the pane into the picture frame using a hot glue gun and glue. Do not place the backing into the frame.

9. Display in front of a window or light to let your design shine!

CIY
STAFF TIP!
You could also make an underwater scene or whatever landscape you'd like to light up!

TURKEY BOWLING

Gobble-gobble! This Turkey Bowling craft is as much fun to make as it is to play! It's game that even the littlest Thanksgiving guest can enjoy.

SUPPLIES:

- Crayola Acrylic Paint
- Disposable plate
- Crayola Paintbrush
- 6 disposable cups
- Crayola No. 2 Pencil
- Crayola Construction Paper
- Crayola Scissors
- Crayola School Glue
- Wiggle eyes
- Crayola Colored Pencils
- Clear tape
- Small ball or plastic pumpkin

STEPS:

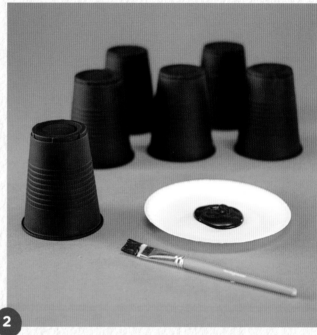

1. Pour brown acrylic paint onto a disposable plate.

2. Using the paintbrush, coat all six cups with a layer of brown paint. Allow the paint to dry completely, and then add a second coat. Allow that to dry for about 1–2 hours.

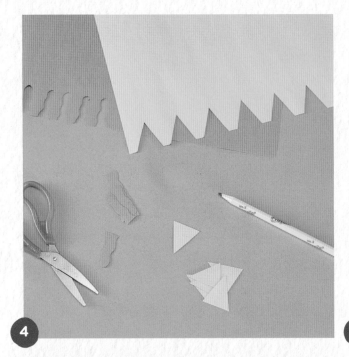

4

5

6

7

3. Using the pencil, draw six triangles onto orange construction paper to make turkey beaks. Cut them out.

4. Draw six squiggly wattles onto red construction paper and cut them out.

5. Glue one beak onto each cup, about one-third of the way from the closed end of the cup. Glue the wattle next to the beak on each turkey cup.

6. Glue a set of wiggle eyes onto each turkey cup. Set aside to let the glue dry.

7. Draw a total of six feathers on different colors of construction paper and cut them out. Decorate them using colored pencils.

8. Tape one feather to the back side of the closed end of a cup. Repeat for all the turkey cups.

9. Set up the turkey cups in one row of three, one row of two, and one row of one. Go bowling for gobblers with a ball or a plastic pumpkin!

THANKSGIVING PLACE CARD HOLDER

Create Thanksgiving place cards and Crayola Model Magic turkeys to hold them for your holiday table. This festive craft will definitely wow the crowd!

HELP FROM ADULTS

Cut the chenille stems in half for younger crafters.

Steph

CIY STAFF TIPS

Create a whole family of turkeys to decorate your Thanksgiving table!

SUPPLIES:

- Crayola Model Magic®
- Wiggle eyes
- Chenille stems
- Crayola Scissors
- Crayola Construction Paper
- Crayola Signature™ Sketch & Detail Dual-Tip Markers
- Crayola Signature™ Gel Pens

STEPS:

1

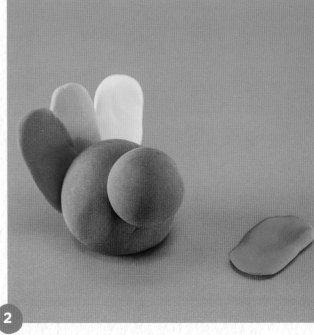

2

1. For each Place Card Holder you want to create, roll brown Crayola Model Magic into one medium and one small ball. Push the balls together to create the body and head of the turkey.

2. Flatten Crayola Model Magic in a variety of colors to create feathers. Attach them to the back of the turkey.

CIY STAFF TIP!

Crayola Model Magic pieces that haven't dried will easily adhere to one another. For added strength, or to attach dried pieces of Crayola Model Magic together, use Crayola Washable No-Run School Glue.

3

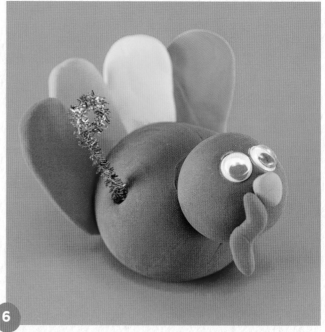

6

7

8

3. Press two wiggle eyes onto the face.

4. Attach a small, triangular piece of orange Crayola Model Magic to create a beak under the eyes.

5. Attach a small, wavy piece of red Model Magic to create the wattle under the beak.

6. Cut chenille stems in half with the scissors so you have one piece for each place card holder. Push one end of the chenille stem into the body of the turkey and curl the other end so it will hold a place card. Allow the turkey to dry overnight.

7. For each place card you want to create, cut out a small rectangular piece of construction paper—about the size of a business card. Use markers to write the names and gel pens to add flourishes.

8. Poke a hole in the bottom of the name tag and place the name tag into the chenille stem holder.

9. Set the place card holders on your Thanksgiving table and get ready to eat!

WINTER

Keep little hands busy and warm with festive winter crafts! Kids can create Thumbprint Holiday Bags and Tags for the giving season, Holiday Ornaments for the tree, and Secret Reveal Valentines for their Valentine's Day pals.

WATERCOLOR-RESIST MITTEN GARLAND

Create this cozy winter mitten garland to hang at home during winter months.

HELP FROM ADULTS

Depending on the age of the kids making this craft, an adult might need to punch the holes in the mittens in step 5.

SUPPLIES:

- Crayola Crayons
- White cardstock
- Crayola Watercolors
- Water
- Disposable cup
- Crayola Paintbrushes
- Crayola Scissors
- Hole punch
- Ribbon

STEPS:

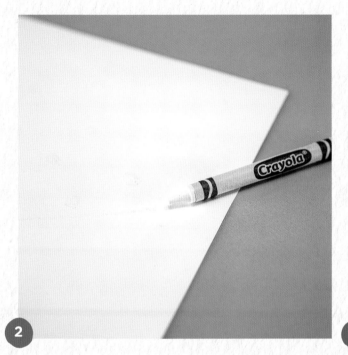

2

3

1. Using a white crayon, draw mitten outlines on the white cardstock.

2. Fill in the mittens with patterns, shapes, and designs, still using the white crayon.

3. Paint over your crayon designs with watercolors to reveal the resist. Allow the paint to dry for 1–2 hours.

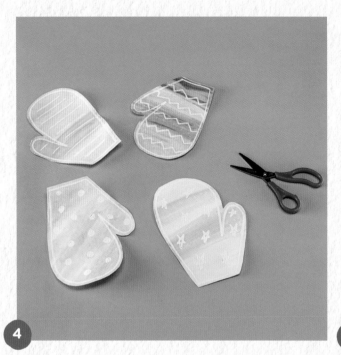

4

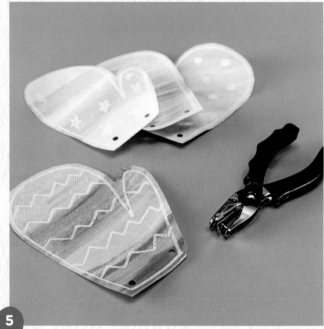

5

4. Cut out the mittens.

5. Punch holes on both sides of the mitten cuff.

6. String a piece of ribbon through the holes and trim the garland to the desired length. Hang and get cozy!

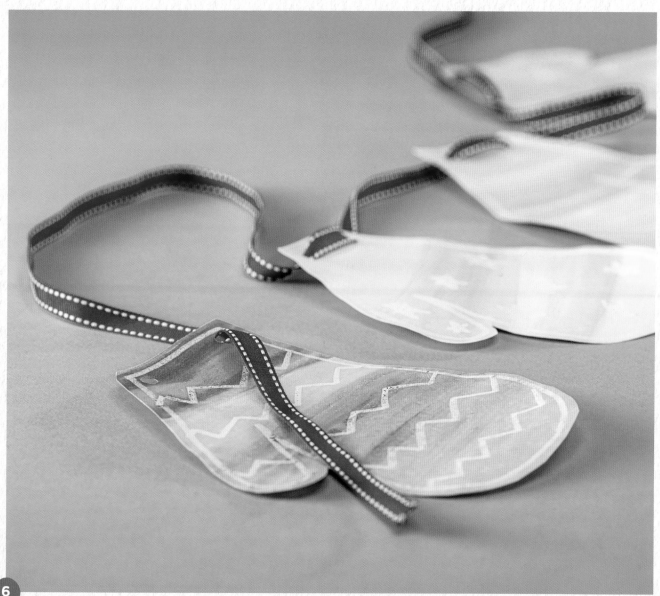

6

SNOWMAN SNOW GLOBE

Sculpt your very own snow globe scene! It's simple to do using Crayola Model Magic and Crayola Glitter Glue!

SUPPLIES:

- Crayola Model Magic®
- Crayola Model Magic® Shape 'n Cut Tools
- Crayola Glitter Glue
- Upcycled jar
- Crayola Paintbrush

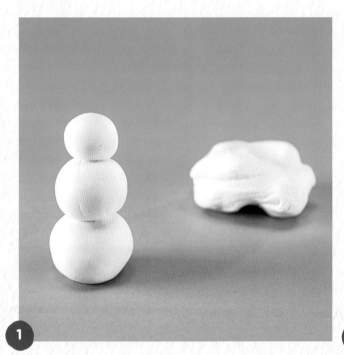

1

2

1. Create three balls using white Crayola Model Magic—small, medium, and large. Stick them together to create a snowman. Brrrr!

2. Use your hand and Crayola Model Magic Shape 'n Cut Tools to help you create details for your snowman out of different colors of Crayola Model Magic, like eyes, a mouth, buttons, a carrot nose, a hat, and a scarf.

CIY STAFF TIP!

Experiment with blending two or more colors of Crayola Model Magic to make a new color.

CIY Staff Tip!

Crayola Model Magic that is fresh from the pack will stick to itself. Dried pieces can be glued together.

3. Draw a generous squiggle of clear glitter glue all around the outside of the jar.

4. Use the paintbrush to spread the clear glitter glue around the outside of the jar.

5

6

5. Add more glittery details with other colors of glitter glue, such as snowflakes or dots. Allow the glue to dry for 3–4 hours.

6. Place the lid of the jar upside-down on a flat surface and put your snowman on the lid. Carefully place the jar over the snowman and twist it into the lid to secure it in place.

CIY STAFF TIP!

For added stability, you can use Crayola Washable No-Run School Glue to adhere your snowman to the lid of the jar.

MARBLEIZED DIY ORNAMENT

You can use Crayola Watercolors and Crayola Washable No-Run School Glue to create a colorful watercolor ornament that is truly unique!

HELP FROM ADULTS

Step 8 may be difficult for little hands, so an adult may want to punch the holes.

SUPPLIES:

- Crayola Watercolors
- Disposable cups
- Warm water
- Craft sticks
- Scrap cardboard
- Wax paper
- Cookie cutter
- Crayola Washable No-Run School Glue
- Straws
- Hole punch
- Ribbon

STEPS:

1. Pop four or five watercolor tablets out of their tray and put each one into its own disposable cup. Add a small amount of warm water and stir with a craft stick until fully dissolved. We used four colors to make our ornament.

2. Lay a piece of cardboard down flat with a sheet of wax paper on top.

3. Place the cookie cutter on the wax paper and pour glue into the cookie cutter until the glue is about $1/4$ inch thick.

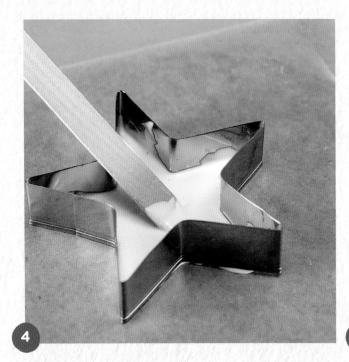

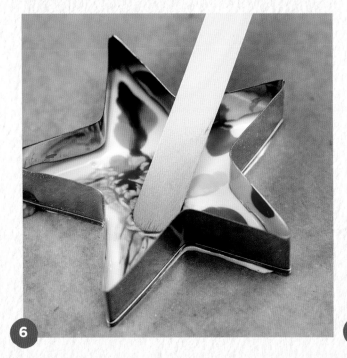

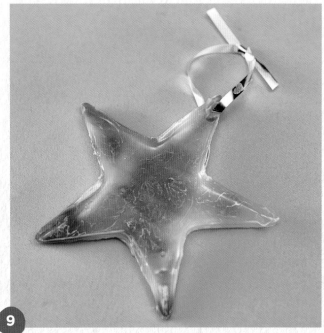

4. Spread the glue evenly with a craft stick.

5. Pull some of the dissolved watercolors into a straw by dipping the straw into the paint solution and then sealing off the top of the straw with your finger. Drip a few drops of each color into the glue.

6. Drag a craft stick through the color drops to create a marbled effect. Allow the glue to dry for 1–2 days.

7. Peel off the wax paper and carefully remove the dried-glue ornament from the cookie cutter.

8. Use the hole punch to create a hole close to the top of the ornament.

9. Loop a ribbon through the hole and tie.

10. Hang the ornament around the house or on your tree!

MELTED CRAYON ORNAMENTS

Melted crayon shavings and a few other supplies can turn mason jar lids into homemade holiday decorations!

HELP FROM ADULTS

Kids will need help with the hair dryer in step 4.

SUPPLIES:

- Crayola Crayons
- Crayola Crayon Sharpener
- Wax paper
- Duct tape
- Hair dryer
- String
- Mason jar lid rings
- Crayola Scissors

STEPS:

1. Unwrap two to six crayons, and use the crayon sharpener to create shavings.

2. Lay a piece of wax paper on a protected surface. Evenly sprinkle the shavings onto the wax paper.

7

8

3. Place a slightly larger piece of wax paper over the shavings and seal the edges with duct tape.

4. Use a hair dryer to melt the shavings. Let cool for 15 minutes.

5. Loop string through the mason jar lid rings and tie the ends together to create the ornament hangers.

6. Use the mason jar lid to trace circles on the wax paper.

7. Cut out the circles. Trim to fit if needed.

8. Carefully press the circles into the back of the mason jar lid.

9. Hang on your tree or anywhere for a bit of holiday cheer!

CIY STAFF TIP!

A pencil sharpener will work if you don't have a crayon sharpener on hand.

HOLIDAY ORNAMENTS

These DIY Crayola Model Magic ornaments are fun and easy holiday crafts for the whole family to create!

CIY STAFF TIPS

Experiment with different winter-themed cookie cutters like a snowman, candy cane, Christmas tree, and more!

SUPPLIES:

- Crayola Model Magic® Shape 'n Cut Tools
- Crayola Model Magic®
- Cookie cutters
- Crayola Scissors
- String

STEPS:

1. Using Crayola Model Magic Shape 'n Cut Tools, roll out Crayola Model Magic to about ½ inch thick on a smooth, flat surface.

2. Use cookie cutters to create the shapes for your ornaments.

CIY STAFF TIP!

We used the end of a Crayola Paintbrush to make the hole in our ornament, but you could use other objects like a paper clip, pencil, or toothpick.

CIY Staff Tip!

Once your ornament has dried completely, you can also decorate it with Crayola Acrylic Paint, Crayola Markers, or Crayola Glitter Glue.

4

5

3. Poke a small hole close to the top of the ornaments.

4. Add decorations and details to your ornaments using different colors of Crayola Model Magic. Allow the ornaments to dry overnight.

5. Cut a piece of string, loop it through the hole in each ornament, and tie a knot.

6. Hang your Crayola Model Magic ornaments around your home or on your tree!

CIY Staff Tip!

Crayola Model Magic that is fresh from the pack will stick to itself. Dried pieces can be glued together.

PAPER QUILL PICTURE FRAME

This fast and easy upcycled craft project turns a cereal box into a super-cool picture frame with paint and paper quill embellishments!

SUPPLIES:

- Ruler
- Crayola No. 2 Pencil
- Empty cereal box
- Crayola Scissors
- Crayola Acrylic Paint
- Crayola Paintbrushes
- Craft stick
- Disposable plate
- Crayola Construction Paper
- Newspaper
- Paper straw
- Crayola Washable No-Run School Glue

STEPS:

1. Using the ruler or another straightedge, draw the outline of a frame on the cereal box with the pencil. It can be any size and thickness you like. Cut out the frame.

2. Paint the plain side of the frame. We mixed together blue and white with a craft stick on a disposable plate to get our color. Let the paint dry for 1–2 hours. Paint a second coat and allow it to dry again for 1–2 hours.

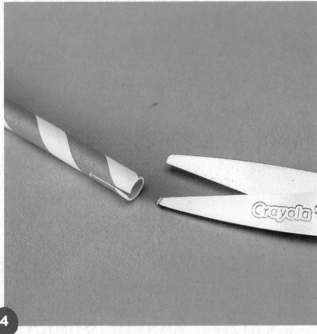

3. While the paint dries, cut different colors of construction paper and a sheet of newspaper into strips about ½ to 1 inch wide. They don't all have to be exactly the same width.

4. Snip a small slit into the paper straw, about ½ to 1 inch long.

CIY STAFF TIP!
Experiment with other colors of paint to customize your picture frame!

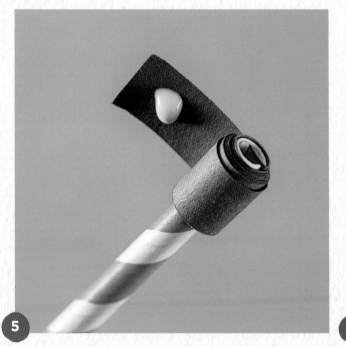

5

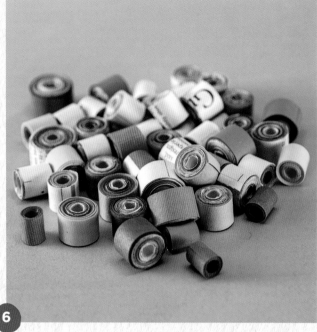

6

5. Slide the end of a construction paper strip into the slit, then wrap it around the straw and glue the end. Slide the quilled paper off of the straw.

6. Repeat step 5 with as many strips of construction paper and newspaper strips as you like, to cover all or part of the frame.

7. Glue the paper quills to the painted frame, let the glue dry, and display!

FAMILY COMMAND CENTER

Make a Family Command Center in your kitchen, office, or anywhere for a little inspiration and to keep busy schedules and tasks organized. This DIY wall setup is easy to make and totally customizable!

HELP FROM ADULTS

Handle the glass for all children, and help little crafters with spelling and penmanship.

-QUOTE OF THE DAY-

SEIZE THE DAY!

SUPPLIES:

- Picture frames with glass
- Crayola Take Note!® Permanent Markers
- Crayola No. 2 Pencil
- Cardstock
- Crayola Scissors
- Ruler
- Crayola Take Note! Dry-Erase Markers

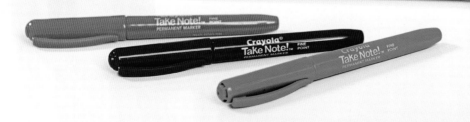

STEPS:

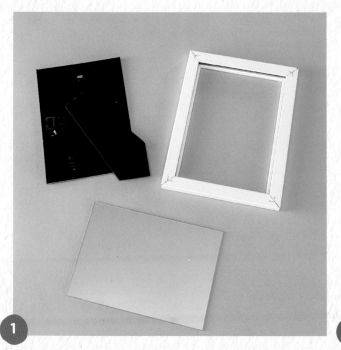

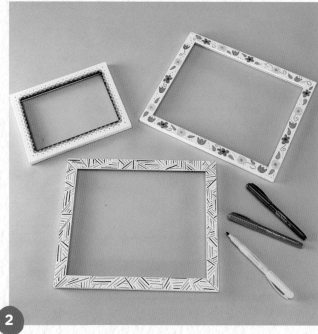

1. Remove the glass from the picture frames and set the glass aside.

2. Using the permanent markers, decorate the picture frames with whatever patterns and themes you like!

3. Using the pencil, trace the inside of the frame onto the cardstock. Cut out the cardstock to fit into the frames.

4. Using permanent markers on the cardstock, write different messages and lists for your command center, such as quotes of the day, a to-do list, a weekly planner, or whatever else would be useful and inspiring to you and your family. Use a ruler to draw lines where needed.

5

6

5. Place the glass back into the frames, then put in your cardstock creations and the frames' backings.

6. Hang your frames where everyone can see them. Keep them up to date using dry-erase markers. What are you up to this week?

CIY STAFF TIP!

Dry-erase markers wipe clean with a paper towel, allowing you to create over and over.

GALAXY PAINT POUR CANVAS

Create cosmically crafty wall art that's out of this world! Turn a plain canvas into a work of art with paint pouring. Attaching a contact paper shape in the middle of your canvas will give a shape that resists paint. When you peel it away, you'll have a space where you can write a far-out message.

SUPPLIES:

- Self-adhesive contact paper
- Crayola Scissors
- Crayola Creativity Canvas
- Crayola Washable Paint
- Disposable cups
- Water
- Craft sticks
- Crayola Paintbrush
- Crayola Markers

STEPS:

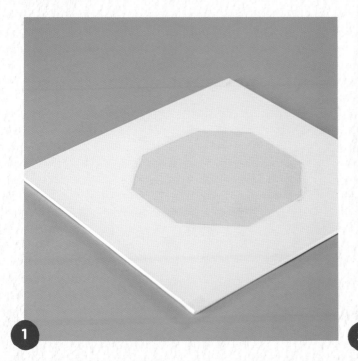

1

2

1. Cut a piece of contact paper into whatever shape you like. We made an octagon. Peel off the backing and attach the shape to the canvas.

2. Pour four or five paint colors into disposable cups, one color per cup.

CIY STAFF TIP!

Paint-and-water mixtures should be smooth but not too watery, just loose enough to pour easily from the cup.

CIY Staff Tip!

If needed, use one or two coats of white Crayola Acrylic Paint to touch up any spots on the edges of the unpainted area.

3

4

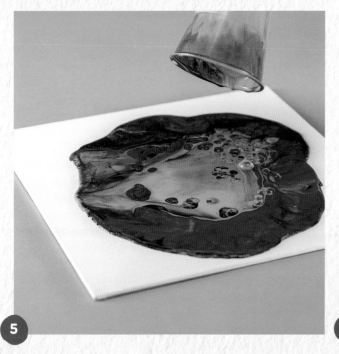

5

6

9

3. Add a little water to the paint and mix it with a craft stick until fully combined. A ratio of about four parts of paint to one part of water should give you a smooth but not runny consistency.

4. In a separate cup, carefully pour in the paint in layers, one color on top of the other. Alternate colors until you have used all of the paint.

5. Over a protected surface, center the canvas on top of the cup. Holding the cup tight to the canvas, flip it over and lay it down flat. Lift the cup straight up and set it aside.

6. Pick up the canvas and gently tilt it from side to side until paint covers the entire canvas. If there are any bare spots, use extra paint from the cup to fill them in.

7. To add accents, dip the paintbrush into a new paint color and flick it at the canvas.

8. Let the paint dry overnight. Check to make sure the paint is entirely dry, then remove the contact paper to reveal the unpainted area.

9. Use markers to write a message in the blank area of your canvas, then display!

VALENTINE'S DAY LANTERN

Sponge-paint a mason jar, decorate it, and add string lights to create a festive Valentine's Day lantern worthy of display!

ADULT SUPERVISION REQUIRED

SUPPLIES:

- Crayola Construction Paper
- Crayola No. 2 Pencil
- Crayola Scissors
- Clear tape
- Mason jar
- Crayola Washable Paint
- Disposable plate
- Sponge or sponge-tipped brush
- Parchment paper
- Battery-operated string lights
- Twine or ribbon

STEPS:

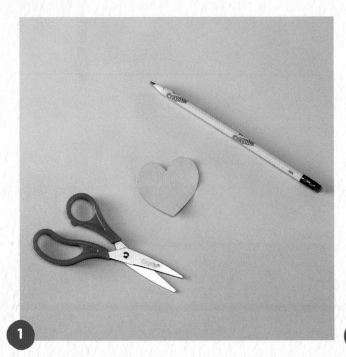

1

2

---

1. First, create a resist (an area impervious to paint) by drawing a heart on construction paper with the pencil and cutting it out.

2. Make a few loops of tape on the back of the paper heart, then tape the paper heart to the outside of the mason jar.

CIY
STAFF TIP!
For extra sparkle, use Crayola Washable Glitter Paint or Crayola Metallic Paint.

3

4

---

3. Pour some paint on the disposable plate. Dip a sponge or sponge-tipped brush into the paint and dab it onto the outside of the mason jar. Let the paint dry for 1–2 hours.

4. When the paint is dry, peel away the heart to reveal the paint resist.

5

7

5. To create a frosted effect, roll up a piece of parchment paper and place it inside the mason jar. Use your fingers to fit it to the inside of your jar.

6. Fill the jar with battery-operated string lights.

7. Add twine or ribbon around the rim of your jar and display!

ICE CUBE PAINTING

This cool twist on Crayola Watercolors turns your watercolor tablets into icy paintbrushes that you can use to create some really chill paintings.

HELP FROM ADULTS

Kids will need help cutting the craft sticks in half in step 4.

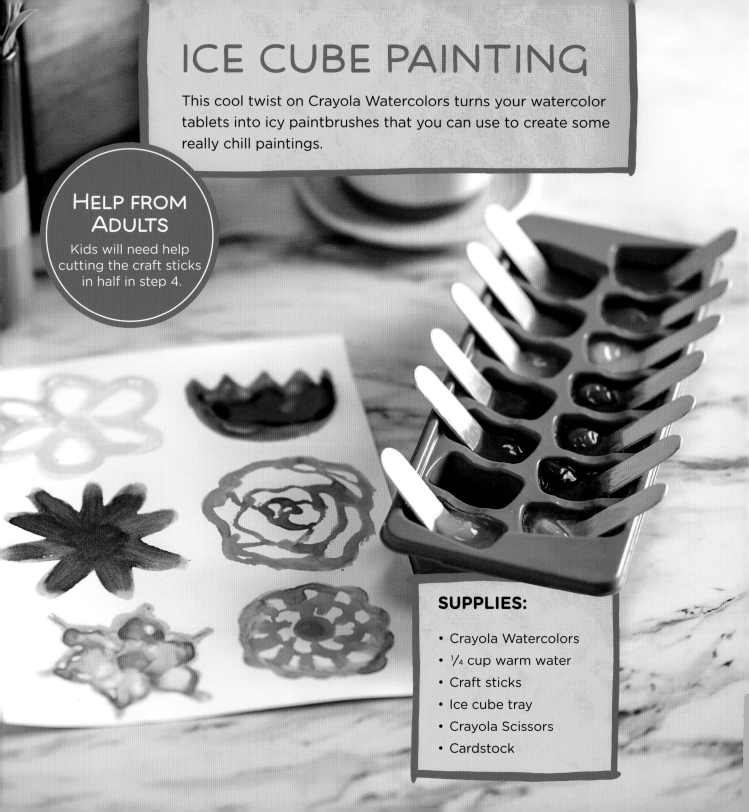

SUPPLIES:

- Crayola Watercolors
- ¼ cup warm water
- Craft sticks
- Ice cube tray
- Crayola Scissors
- Cardstock

STEPS:

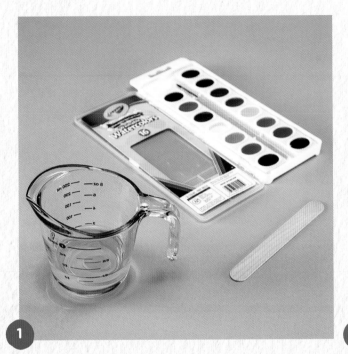

1

2

1. Place a watercolor tablet in ¼ cup of warm water and mix with a craft stick until it dissolves.

2. Pour the mixture into the ice cube tray.

CIY STAFF TIP!
You can make new colors by mixing together the liquified paint before you freeze it.

CIY STAFF TIP!

Flip this project around and let kids paint on ice! Freeze a cake pan full of water and paint on it as usual using watercolors to create bright works of art that melt away before your eyes.

3

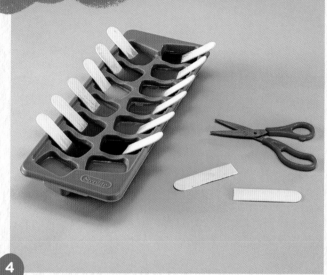

4

3. Repeat with as many colors as you like.

4. Cut craft sticks in half so you have half of a craft stick for every color. Place a craft stick half, cut end down, into each cavity with paint in it in your ice cube tray. Freeze for 5-6 hours.

5. Use your frozen paint cubes like paint brushes to create colorful patterns and pictures on the cardstock.

SECRET REVEAL VALENTINES

Kids can surprise friends and classmates with secret Valentine messages! White crayons can be used to create designs on DIY Valentine's Day cards that are magically revealed with watercolors.

SUPPLIES:

- Crayola No. 2 Pencil
- Cardstock
- Crayola Crayons
- Crayola Scissors
- Envelopes
- Crayola Watercolors

STEPS:

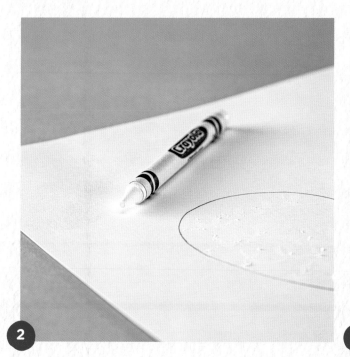

2

3

1. Lightly draw the outline of a heart with a pencil on cardstock.

2. Use a white crayon to create your secret designs, messages, and names on the card.

3. Use colored crayons to decorate the card with designs and words you want the recipient to see before they reveal the secret message.

4. Cut out the heart shape using scissors.

5. Place each card in an envelope and hand them out to friends, letting them know to use watercolors to reveal the secret. You can even give watercolor paint along with the card as a Valentine's Day gift.

6. Recipients paint over the card using watercolors to reveal the secret Valentine designs and messages!

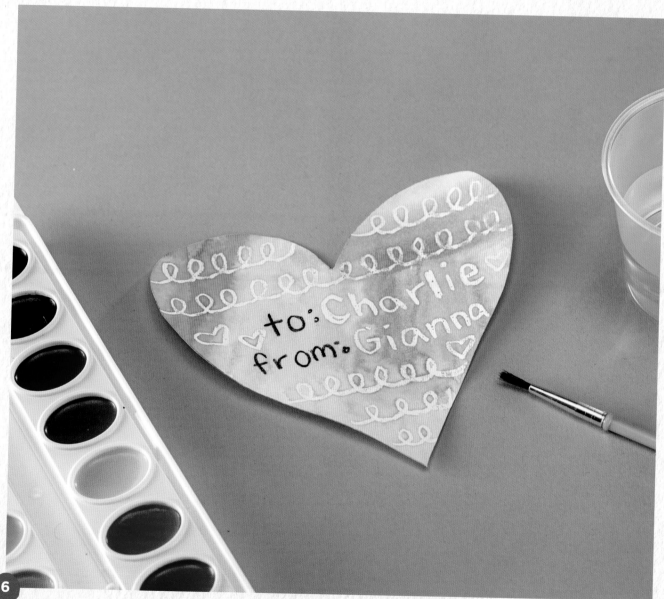

6

DIY STICKERS

Kids can add some personalized flare just about anywhere with these homemade stickers.

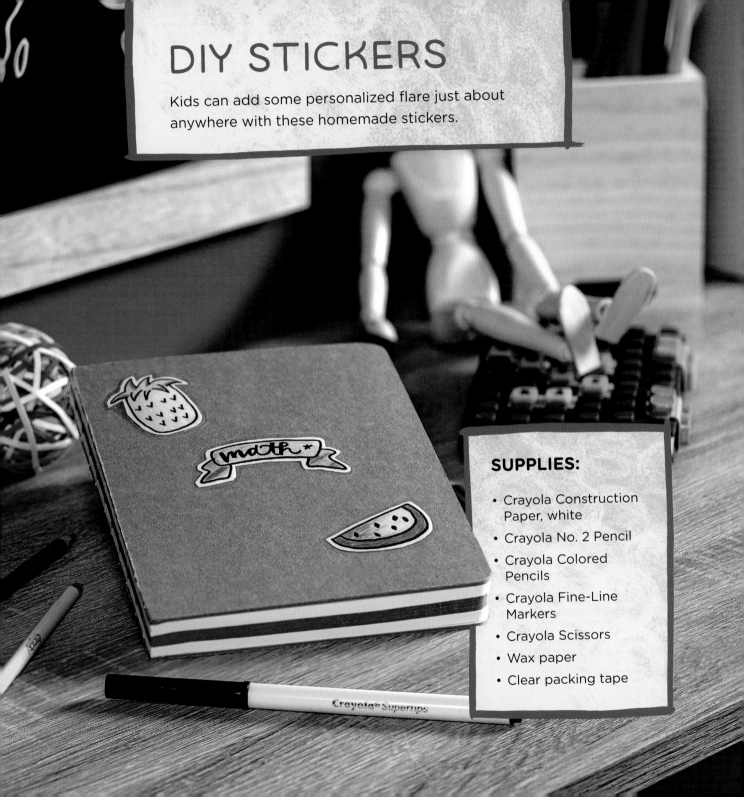

SUPPLIES:

- Crayola Construction Paper, white
- Crayola No. 2 Pencil
- Crayola Colored Pencils
- Crayola Fine-Line Markers
- Crayola Scissors
- Wax paper
- Clear packing tape

STEPS:

1. On a piece of white construction paper, draw the outlines of some fun shapes with the pencil. We drew a pineapple, a slice of watermelon, and a banner.

2. Using colored pencils, color in your designs.

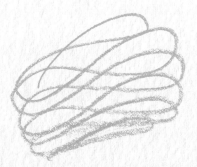

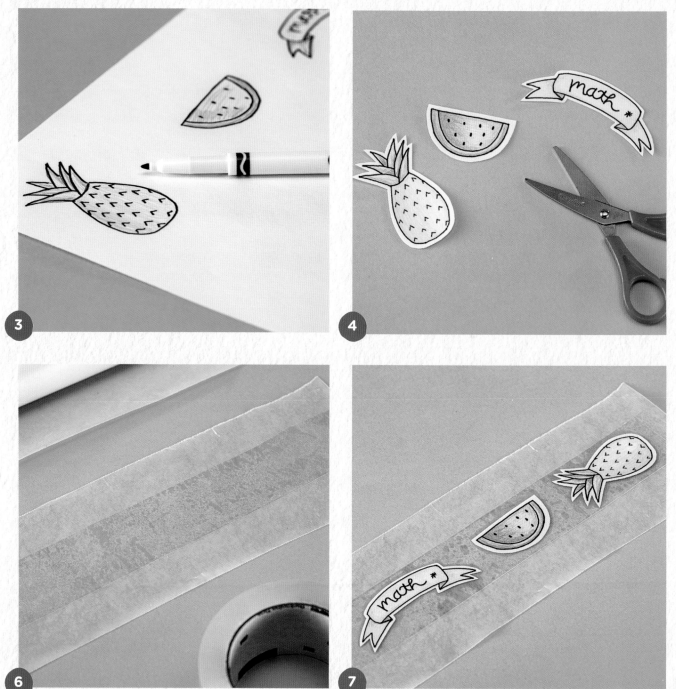

8

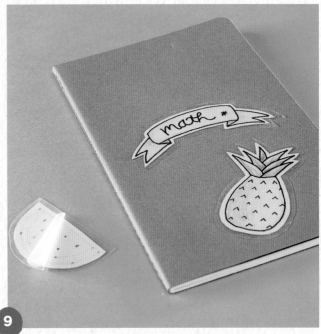

9

3. Go over the edges and details of the drawings using the fine-line markers.

4. Cut out the designs, leaving a bit of white around the edges.

5. Lay a piece of wax paper down flat.

6. Tape a strip of packing tape to the wax paper, sticky side down.

7. Place the drawings on the tape, then put another layer of tape on top of them.

8. Cut out the drawings, leaving a bit of the wax paper and tape around the edges.

9. To decorate using your personalized stickers, just peel off the wax paper and stick away!

THUMBPRINT HOLIDAY BAGS AND TAGS

Make personalized gift bags and tags that literally have your fingerprints all over them!

SUPPLIES:

- Crayola Super Tips Markers
- Paper gift bags
- Crayola Washable Paint
- Disposable plates
- Paper gift tags
- Crayola Glitter Glue

TO: steph
FROM: Alisha